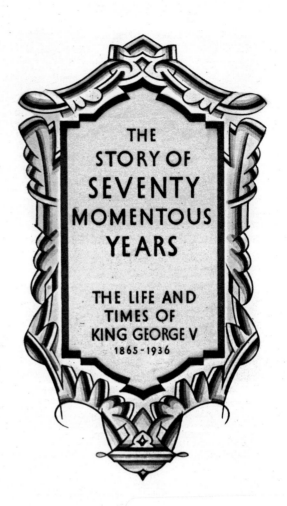

THE
STORY OF
**SEVENTY
MOMENTOUS
YEARS**

THE LIFE AND
TIMES OF
KING GEORGE V
1865-1936

Photo: *Vandyk*

HIS MAJESTY KING GEORGE V

1865—1936

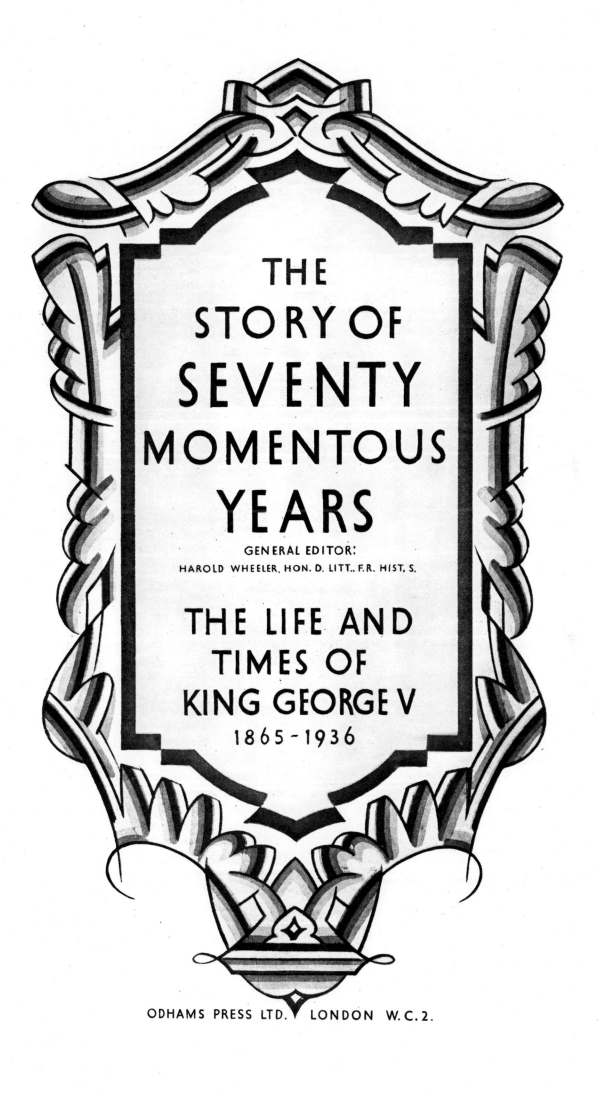

THE STORY OF SEVENTY MOMENTOUS YEARS

GENERAL EDITOR:
HAROLD WHEELER, HON. D. LITT., F.R. HIST. S.

THE LIFE AND TIMES OF KING GEORGE V
1865 - 1936

ODHAMS PRESS LTD. LONDON W.C. 2.

QUEEN MARY'S MESSAGE TO HER PEOPLE

"I MUST send to you, the people of this nation and Empire, a message of my deepest gratitude for all the sympathy with which, at this time of sorrow, you have surrounded me.

"It is indeed a gratitude so deep that I cannot find words to express it. But the simplest words are the best. I can only say—with all my heart, I thank you.

"In my own great sorrow I have been upheld not only by the strength of your sympathy but also by the knowledge that you have shared my grief.

"For I have been deeply moved by the signs so full and touching that the passing of my dear husband has brought a real sense of personal sorrow to all his subjects.

"In the midst of my grief I rejoice to think that after his Reign of twenty-five years he lived to know that he had received the reward in overflowing measure of the loyalty and love of his people.

"Although he will be no longer at my side—and no words can tell how I shall miss him—I trust that with God's help I may still be able to continue some part at least of the service which for forty-two years of happy married life we tried together to give to this great land and empire.

"During the coming years, with all the changes which they must bring, you will, I know, let me have a place in your thoughts and prayers.

"I commend to you my dear son as he enters upon his Reign, in confident hope that you will give to him the same devotion and loyalty which you gave so abundantly to his father.

"God bless you, dear people, for all the wonderful love and sympathy with which you have sustained me."

MARY

HIS MAJESTY KING GEORGE V

THE ADDRESS GIVEN BY

HIS GRACE THE LORD ARCHBISHOP OF CANTERBURY

IN WESTMINSTER ABBEY, ON SUNDAY, JANUARY 26th, 1936
IS REPRODUCED BY SPECIAL PERMISSION AS A
FOREWORD TO THIS VOLUME

" O man, greatly beloved, peace be unto thee "
Daniel x, 19.

IT is perhaps not easy for us under the pressure of a great immediate sorrow to foresee what place the verdict of history will give to King George V in the long line of British Kings. Yet I venture to predict that that verdict will confirm the simple, spontaneous judgment expressed last week by a workman at my Lambeth home: "We never had a better."

Assuredly there have been Kings and Queens more powerful, more forcible, more romantic in the circumstances of their lives, and who have exercised a more commanding influence on the public affairs of their time. Yet here, in the region of public influence, the future historian must give a high place to King George. For he will see more clearly than we can that his reign was marked by changes, in the extension of the franchise, and in the Constitution of the Realm and the Empire, more far-reaching than in almost any previous reign; and that through all these changes the position of the Monarchy was not only maintained but strengthened. He will recognize that this could not have been possible unless the King himself had been a man of most marked tact and self-control and resolute loyalty to the principles of Constitutional government. The historian will be the more impressed because the memorials of King George which he will possess will show him to have been a man of strong personal opinions, wont to express them to his friends in singularly forcible terms. The historian will record that, while either personal weakness or self-assertion would have endangered the Monarchy, the mingled strength and self-restraint of King George made it stronger than ever before.

THE KING'S INFLUENCE

In the second place our historian will most certainly record that these 25 years, including as they did the Great War and all the economic disorders which followed it, put the spirit of the British people to a severer test than at any other time in their history. When he asks how it was that the people kept so united, so resolute, his inquiry will bring him to the influence of the King, who in the midst of all anxieties stood himself so steadfast and confident and courageous that he became the symbol and centre of the nation's unity and strength. Yes, even when he measures by these tests of beneficent public influence will not the historian be bound to ask, "After all, has Britain ever had a better King? "

But to us, his contemporaries, his own subjects, the title of King George to a place among the best of British Kings rests upon a surer, deeper basis. It is that he was a man greatly beloved. Of that fact there can be no doubt. The celebrations of the Silver Jubilee year and the solemnities of this last week are overwhelming evidence. Make all allowances for the new powers of publicity, with their undoubted effect in creating mass emotion; is there record in our history of any such demonstration, so spontaneous, so universal, of a great stirring of the common heart?

I remember well the funeral of Queen Victoria, as I was privileged to take a part, small, but to me most moving. It was beyond all words impressive—the little yacht bearing the Queen's body passing through the lines of great battleships as they thundered their last salute, and coming to anchor as the winter sun set in a blaze of crimson and gold; the vast crowds lining the shores; next day the procession moving through the streets of London in a silence that could be felt. It was reverence for the great Queen and a sense almost of awe at the passing of a great epoch that moved the multitude.

I remember also the funeral of King Edward VII, and the genuine sorrow at the vanishing from our sight of a King so gracious, so full of charm, vitality, and rich humanity. But I cannot remember in either case just this all-pervading sense of personal bereavement springing from a sense of personal affection.

THE KING'S PERSONALITY

The long lines of people who have been passing the body of King George as it lies in the silent storied spaces of Westminster Hall must have felt, "Here lies a man greatly beloved." We never had a better King, because never a King more loved by his people.

Of the fact there can be no doubt; but how is it to be explained? The question is more easily asked than answered. King George himself, speaking to me about all those overwhelming evidences of loyalty which the Silver Jubilee called forth, used some words so characteristic of his honesty and humility that I cannot refrain from repeating them even in these surroundings. I seem to hear him say them now. "I am sure I cannot understand it, for, after all, I am only a very ordinary sort of fellow." There was a truth in those simple words which he himself could not discern, for the secret of the power of his personality over his people was, I think, as I have said elsewhere, that they came to see in him just the sort of man each of them instinctively would wish to be—simple, sincere, frank, a lover of home and of healthy sport, loyal to his friends, keeping a high standard of personal life and public duty, steadfast in service, and mindful of his God. Such a man his people understood. They saw in him the simple sterling virtues which each of them knew to be right for himself. This was the personality which more and more fully as the years passed communicated itself to the people.

In the later time of his life he was enabled by the marvellous invention of the wireless to come into direct touch with them all throughout every part of his far-reaching Empire. When they heard his own voice and the simple, strong, sincere words he spoke, they felt more than ever he was in the best sense one of themselves, that they belonged to each other, bound by ties of mutual understanding and trust, and that he was a true father of them all.

THE KING'S RELIGION

Beneath this personality, which thus gradually and surely became so greatly beloved, was a foundation which in this place, this central shrine of our national Christianity, must be specially remembered. It was his religion. There are only two words needed to describe King George's religion. It was simple. It was real. Simple certainly. There were great and rich regions of religion to which he was a comparative stranger; ecclesiastical, emotional, sacramental, mystical. His religion was based on an all-abiding sense of his responsibility and his duty to God. If we use the old words, the fear of God, in their true Bible sense, as a reverent remembrance of God's reality and claim, King George was a God-fearing man. A simple religion, but very real. It was expressed in certain habits of life of which he said little, but which he resolutely kept—his daily prayers, his daily reading of the Bible—I doubt whether any layman had a more accurate, if not always fully instructed, knowledge of the Bible—Sunday after Sunday, wherever he might be, his presence at the public worship of God.

I cannot but remember at this moment that twenty-four years ago, at his Coronation, speaking from this place. I tried in a few words to describe the true sovereignty of service. He lived to wield that sovereignty most fully. I am sure that it was in his deep sense of responsibility to God that he found the motive and the support for his sense of responsibility to the nation and for his unwearying service. To the very end he was unswerving in his devotion to duty. It may be that some of you have read the description I ventured to give to the House of Lords last Thursday of his very last public act, a few hours before his death—that last most pathetic but most gallant rally to the old claim of duty. Deep down in that inner region where dwell the ultimate motives of life his duty to God stood strong. However limited a religion so simple may seem to be, it met the great requirement of all religion, to do justly, to love mercy, and to walk humbly with God.

THE KING'S EXAMPLE

So he has passed from us—this man greatly beloved. God bless him and keep him. But are we content to let him pass into the silence leaving nothing but a memory behind? Must not our love and loyalty bid us not only keep his memory within us but also keep his example before us? Through that example, "he, being dead, yet speaketh," and the voice which had become so familiar to us can still be heard. Mindful of that example, let me, as I close, ask two things of you, his people, while your hearts are stilled and solemnized by sorrow.

The first is this: recover simplicity of life. It is a phrase often used to advocate all sorts of artificial contrivances, but the true simplification of life must come from within, from the region of the soul. Truly it is needed. For a hundred reasons our modern life is becoming increasingly complicated, tangled, confused. We have need to recover those old, strong, sterling virtues to which our nation and every nation has given homage in the homage that was given to King George. In the midst of the whirl of amusements keep a steadying rule of duty. In the midst of all temptations to selfishness, to get for ourselves all that life can bring us, keep a place for some disinterested service to others, especially to those to whom life seems to bring so little; let service come before self. While marriage is being treated with so much recklessness and frivolity, remember the home life of King George, and keep your own homes pure and stable. When a hundred voices in fiction, in the Press, and in talk are muddling and confusing conscience, set before yourselves some fixed standard of personal integrity and honour below which you will scorn to fall. Prove in your own lives what King George proved in his: that simplicity is strength.

And let none think that this discipline will deprive life of its true pleasures. It will but clear away the weeds. With all his self-discipline King George himself loved life and sport and laughter. It is always for the true of heart that there springs up joyful gladness. Fundamental truth of heart —that is our need.

"LEST WE FORGET"

The second thing I would ask of you for his sake is—recover remembrance of God. In the ever-increasing speed of mere physical movement, "faster and faster" seems to be becoming almost a motto of existence. The haste and hurry and distraction of life infects the soul. In the mere jostle of sensations and of opinions we have no time to stop and think, and God is crowded out. Yet it is sternly true that without some inner hold on God within neither man nor nation can be stable and strong. Let us take heed to the warning uttered in the days of our prosperity by that poet and prophet whose ashes have just been buried beneath the floor of this Abbey Church—

Lord God of Hosts, be with us yet
Lest we forget—lest we forget.

Let the steadfast, God-fearing King speak to us from the world of eternal truth into which he has passed. "O my people, remember, remember the Lord God of your Fathers."

For us still the struggle, wherein his example may quiet us, steady us and keep us true; for him the eternal rest. As on Tuesday morning I looked for the last time upon the face of my King, my friend, and wondered at the light of beautiful serenity which lay upon it, it seemed to me as if a greeting had already come to him from beyond the veil:—"O man greatly beloved, peace be to thee."

The original text reproduced by courtesy of "*The Times*."

QUEEN VICTORIA = PRINCE ALBERT OF SAXE-COBURG AND GOTHA, PRINCE CONSORT,
b. May 24, 1819. acceded, June 20, 1837. d. Jan. 22, 1901. Reigned 63 years 7 months
b. Aug. 26, 1819. d. Dec. 14, 1861.

VICTORIA PRINCESS ROYAL (d. 1901) (m. Frederick III German Emperor and King of Prussia who d. 1888)
WILLIAM II (b. 1859 German Emperor and King of Prussia, 1888-1918) (m. 1st, Augusta of Schleswig-Holstein-Sonderburg-Augustenburg, (has issue); 2nd, Princess Hermine of Reuss)

EDWARD VII (b. Nov. 9, 1841, acceded, Jan. 22, 1901. d. May 6, 1910) (m. PRINCESS ALEXANDRA OF DENMARK on March 10, 1863, who d. Nov. 20, 1925)

ALICE (d. 1878) (m. Ernest Louis Grand Duke of Hesse)

ALFRED, DUKE OF EDINBURGH (d. 1900) (m. Grand Duchess Marie of Russia, who d. 1920)
3 SONS

HELENA (d. 1923) (m. Prince Christian of Schleswig-Holstein who d. 1917)
HELENA VICTORIA (b. 1870) MARIE LOUISE (b. 1872) (m. Prince Aribert of Anhalt who d. 1933)

LOUISE (b. 1848) (m. Duke of Argyll who d. 1914)

ARTHUR, DUKE OF CONNAUGHT (b. 1850) (m. Princess Louise of Prussia who d. 1917)

LEOPOLD, DUKE OF ALBANY (d. 1884) (m. Princess Helena of Waldeck-Pyrmont)
ALICE (b. 1883) (m. Earl of Athlone) CHARLES EDWARD DUKE OF SAXE-COBURG AND GOTHA (b. 1884) (m. Princess Victoria of Schleswig-Holstein-Sonderburg-Glücksburg)

BEATRICE (b. 1857) (m. Prince Henry of Battenberg, who d. 1896)

ALBERT, DUKE OF CLARENCE (d. 1892)

GEORGE V (b. June 3, 1865. acceded, May 6, 1910. d. Jan. 20, 1936) (m. on July 6, 1893, PRINCESS MARY OF TECK b. May 26, 1867)

LOUISE PRINCESS ROYAL (d. 1931) (m. Duke of Fife who d. 1912)
ALEXANDRA DUCHESS OF FIFE (b. 1891) (m. Prince Arthur of Connaught) MAUD (b. 1893) (m. Lord Carnegie)

VICTORIA (d. 1935)

MAUD (b. 1869) (m. King Haakon VII of Norway)

MARGARET (d. 1920) (m. Gustavus Adolphus Crown Prince of Sweden)
ARTHUR (b. 1883) (m. Alexandra Duchess of Fife)
PATRICIA (b. 1886) (m. Vice-Adm. Hon. Sir Alexander Ramsay)
ALASTAIR, EARL OF MACDUFF (b. 1914)

EDWARD VIII (b. June 23, 1894. acceded Jan. 20 1936)

ALBERT, DUKE OF YORK (b. 1895) (m. Lady Elizabeth Bowes-Lyon)
ELIZABETH (b. 1926) MARGARET ROSE (b. 1930)

MARY PRINCESS ROYAL (b. 1897) (m. Earl of Harewood)
GEORGE VISCOUNT LASCELLES (b. 1923) GERALD (b. 1924)

HENRY, DUKE OF GLOUCESTER (b. 1900) (m. Lady Alice Montagu-Douglas-Scott)

GEORGE, DUKE OF KENT (b. 1902) (m. Princess Marina of Greece)
EDWARD (b. 1935)

JOHN (d. 1919)

VICTORIA EUGÉNIE (Ena) (b. 1887) (m. King Alfonso of Spain)
ALEXANDER, MARQUESS OF CARISBROOKE (b. 1886) (m. Lady Irene Denison, daughter of William, 2nd Earl of Londesborough)
LEOPOLD (d. 1922)

MAURICE (d. 1914)

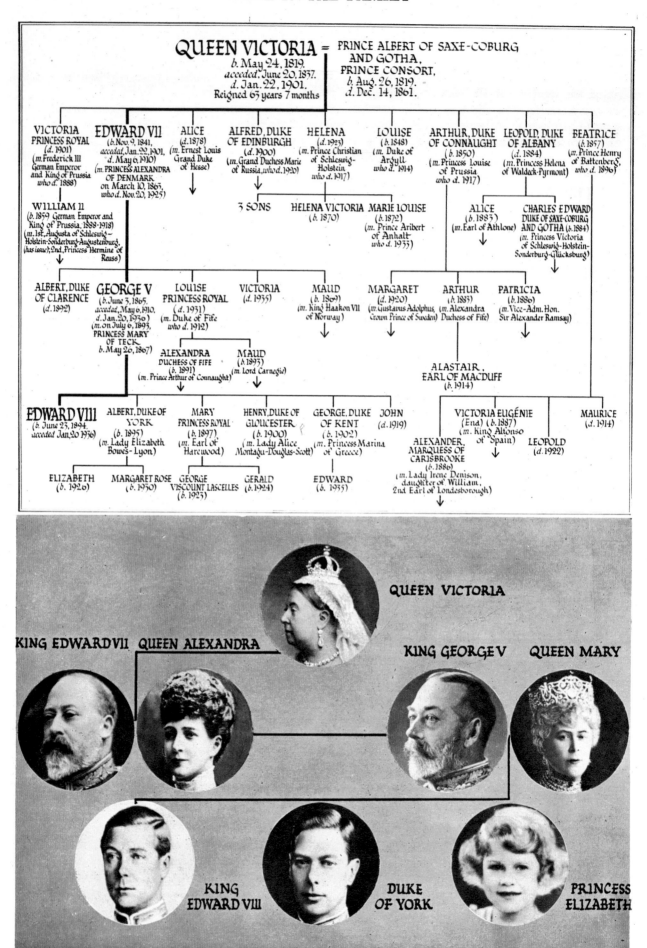

QUEEN VICTORIA

KING EDWARD VII   QUEEN ALEXANDRA   KING GEORGE V   QUEEN MARY

KING EDWARD VIII   DUKE OF YORK   PRINCESS ELIZABETH

Photos : Elliott & Fry and Bassano

King George V was born at Marlborough House, London, on June 3, 1865, the second son of King Edward VII and Queen Alexandra, who were then Prince and Princess of Wales, an elder brother, Prince Albert Victor, having been born on January 8, 1864. Our pictures show Prince George at the age of two, five, eight, and eleven years.

Photo : W. & D. Downey

After receiving a good all-round education from the Rev. (later Canon) J. N. Dalton, curate of Sandringham, young Prince George, with his elder brother, Prince Albert Victor, afterwards Duke of Clarence, was sent as a naval cadet to the *Britannia*. He joined the ship just after his twelfth birthday, and was rated midshipman on January 8, 1880.

A Royal Family group. From left to right : The Duke of Clarence, Princess Maud, later Queen of Norway, the Princess of Wales, Princess Louise, afterwards Duchess of Fife, the Prince of Wales, Prince George and Princess Victoria. On January 14, 1892, the family circle was broken by the sudden death of the Duke of Clarence, and Prince George succeeded his brother as second in the direct line of succession to the throne.

Photo : Topical

Created Duke of York in 1892, the future King retained his keen interest in sea affairs, kindled by long cruises in the *Bacchante* between 1879 and 1882. He had received his first independent command in 1889, and was promoted captain in 1893.

Photo : F. G. O. Stuart

In May, 1893, the betrothal of the Duke of York to Princess Victoria Mary, daughter of the Duke and Duchess of Teck, was announced. The bride-to-be, generally known as "Princess May," was popular, and there was an added satisfaction in the fact that for the first time in 200 years an English princess was to wed an heir to the throne.

Photo : Fox

The marriage of the Duke of York and Princess Victoria Mary took place on July 6, 1893, in the Chapel Royal of St. James's Palace, before a distinguished gathering of British and foreign royalty. All England made holiday, while later thousands of people thronged to the Imperial Institute, where the wedding presents, over 3,500 in number, were on view.

Photo : W. & D. Downey

FOUR GENERATIONS

Photo : W. & D. Downey

On June 23, 1894, a son was born to the Duke and Duchess of York at White Lodge, Richmond, which had become one of the residences of the royal couple on their marriage. The infant, now King Edward VIII, was christened Edward Albert Christian George Andrew Patrick David. A second son, the present Duke of York, was born in December, 1895. The four monarchs shown on this page cover a period of almost one hundred years.

A view of Regent Street during "the Season" of 1865.

During the last years of the 'sixties the crinoline, which had grown to vast proportions, disappeared to give place to the narrow bustle. The top right photograph was taken about 1876. The bottom left-hand picture shows a frock of the early 'seventies. Below (right) is an elegant plate of 1878. Inset, a coquettish hat of 1866.

FASHIONS IN THE 'EIGHTIES AND 'NINETIES

In the 'eighties a wider silhouette became the mode. The bustle was reaching its climax. The bottom picture shows some of the more graceful fashions of the period. The sweeping lines developed into the less pleasing forms shown in the top picture. Note the three-quarter length cape or dolmen and the peculiar over-ornamented straw hats.

(1) Nellie Melba, the "Australian Nightingale"; (2) Madame Patti, a popular prima donna; (3) Arthur Roberts, a famous comedian; (4) Sir William Schwenk Gilbert who collaborated for many years with (5) Sir Arthur Sullivan, in the production of the Savoy operas; (6) Sir Henry Irving, the great actor; (7) Nellie Farren, the music hall artiste; and (8) Ellen Terry, one of the most distinguished English actresses of all times.

(1) Bob Fitzsimmons, the famous boxer; (2) W. I. Bassett, the great English international footballer, who played for West Bromwich Albion; (3) Capt. Webb, the first man to swim the Channel (1875); (4) Fred Archer, champion jockey of his day; (5) H. L. Doherty, lawn tennis champion; (6) W. G. Grace, the Grand Old Man of cricket; (7) the winning Oxford boat crew of 1896—between 1890 and 1898 Oxford won the boat race nine times in succession.

Illustrations : 5, courtesy " The Autocar." 6, courtesy Southern Railway

Quaint vehicles were produced in the search for more speed. Here we illustrate (1) a " penny-farthing " bicycle; (2) a " phantom " bicycle, patented in 1869; (3) an old horsebrake; (4) the craze for cycling which came with the safety bicycle; (5) an early type of motor car in 1898; and (6) an express engine, the Sybil, built in 1868 for the L.S.W.R.

Here are shown (1) a Packard car of 1897; (2) the first licensed hackney carriage in England (1898); (3) a horse tram of this period side by side with (4) the first motor bus in London of the Lawson type (1899); and (5) a typical traffic scene outside Charing Cross Station in 1880 before the appearance of the new means of transport.

(1) W. E. Gladstone; (2) Benjamin Disraeli, Lord Beaconsfield; (3) Garibaldi, Italian patriot; (4) William Booth, founder of the Salvation Army; (5) David Livingstone, African explorer; (6) The Rev. C. H. Spurgeon, famous preacher; (7) Thomas A. Edison, inventor of the gramophone; (8) Alexander Graham Bell, inventor of the telephone; (9) Gottlieb Daimler, pioneer of the petrol engine; (10) General Gordon; (11) Florence Nightingale, heroine of the Crimea, and founder of many institutes for training nurses; (12) Sir Isaac Pitman, inventor of a shorthand system.

(1) Charles Dickens, famous novelist; (2) R. L. Stevenson, novelist and essayist; (3) Thomas Carlyle, philosopher, historian, and political writer; (4) Charles Darwin, scientist and naturalist; (5) "George Eliot," celebrated novelist; (6) Karl Marx, author of *Das Kapital;* (7) Alfred, Lord Tennyson, Poet Laureate; (8) Robert Browning, poet; (9) Richard Wagner, composer; (10) Marie Rosalie (Rosa) Bonheur, French animal painter; (11) Sir Edwin Landseer, the famous English animal painter; (12) Johanna Maria (Jenny) Lind, the " Swedish Nightingale."

Few events in Queen Victoria's long reign exceeded in magnificence and sincerity of feeling the brilliant Diamond Jubilee celebration of 1897. Every section of the Empire was represented in the glittering procession which on June 22 made its way from Buckingham Palace to St. Paul's Cathedral. Just before entering her carriage the aged queen, who had become an almost legendary figure in the minds of millions of her subjects, sent a message saying, "From my heart I thank my beloved people. May God bless them."

Photo : Fox

Scarcely had the echoes of the Jubilee died away before Great Britain was involved in hostilities in South Africa. On October 11, 1899, after the failure of a conference at Bloemfontein, war broke out between the British Empire and the Boer Republics of Transvaal and the Orange Free State, and was followed immediately by Boer invasions of British territory

Photo : Horace W. Nicholls

At first the campaign went badly for Britain : Ladysmith, Mafeking, and Kimberley were invested, and British columns sent to their relief suffered grievously from heat, from sickness, and at the hands of foes who knew every inch of the ground, were superb marksmen, and were admirably led by men such as Louis Botha, Jan Christian Smuts, and Christian de Wet.

Photo : Horace W. Nicholls

The years 1901 and 1902 were occupied in guerilla warfare in which armoured trains and cars, flying columns and ambuscades played a prominent part.   After the loss of nearly 20,000 British lives peace was signed on May 31, 1902.

Photo : Illustrated London News

The tide turned when Lord Roberts was put in command with Lord Kitchener as chief of staff.   The relief of Mafeking, which had been defended by Colonel (later Lord) Baden-Powell, on May 17, 1900, was the occasion of tumultous rejoicing throughout Britain.   Hence the addition of the words maffick, mafficker, and mafficking to the language.

Left, reading downwards : The Marquis of Salisbury, Prime Minister throughout the war; Sir Alfred (later Lord) Milner, who was appointed Governor of Cape Colony in 1897, to investigate the trouble then brewing. Sir Redvers Buller relieved Ladysmith on February 28, 1900. Centre : Lord Roberts, appointed to supreme command after a serious repulse in December, 1899. Right, reading downwards : Lord Kitchener, Chief of Staff to Roberts and later Commander-in-chief. Paul Kruger, President of the Transvaal Republic from 1883 to 1900, when he left the country following the fall of Pretoria. Making his way to Europe, he settled in Holland after making an unsuccessful appeal to various Powers to use their influence on behalf of the Boers; Christian de Wet, the most skilful and daring of the Boer guerilla leaders, and the only one who remained undefeated at the end of the war.

Photos : Central News, Elliott & Fry & Horace W. Nicholls.

Photo : Elliott & Fry

Public anxieties and private griefs clouded the last days of Queen Victoria, who died on January 22, 1901. Her subjects, most of whom had known no other ruler, mourned the loss as a personal affliction, and her death marked the end of an epoch. She died at Osborne House, Isle of Wight, and her coffin was placed in the mausoleum at Frogmore.

Photo : Horace W. Nicholls

One of Queen Victoria's last acts was to arrange for the Duke of York to visit Australia to open the first Federal Parliament of the Commonwealth which came into being on January 1, 1901. On March 16, 1901, the Duke and Duchess left Portsmouth on the *Ophir*. During their tour they visited South Africa, Canada, and Newfoundland.

The coronation of King Edward VII, originally fixed for June 26, 1902, had at the last moment to be postponed. O
Tuesday, June 24, London was changed in an instant from a city of rejoicing to one of gloom by the announcement that a
operation on His Majesty was being performed, and for a week the King's life was in danger. Thanks to the skill of h

Photo : *Topical*

edical attendants and the devoted nursing of Queen Alexandra he recovered rapidly, and after a brief tour on the royal
cht returned to London for his coronation which took place on August 9. The conclusion of the South African War
the signing of the Peace of Pretoria on May 31, 1902, was a happy inauguration to the reign of King Edward VII.

Photo : Photopress

While peace reigned in Europe war broke out between Russia and Japan over Manchuria and Korea. In February, 1904, the Japanese successfully attacked the Russian fleet outside Port Arthur, which, after a long siege, surrendered on January 2, 1905, its fall being largely due to the strict blockade maintained by Admiral Togo, seen above.

(1) H. G. Pelissier, founder of the Follies, an original theatrical troupe. (2) Madame Tetrazzini, Italian prima donna. (3) Enrico Caruso, prince of tenors. (4) Sara Bernhardt, for many years queen of the stage. (5) Dan Leno, quaintest of comedians. (6) Marie Lloyd, idol of the Cockney. (7) Sir Herbert Beerbohm Tree, actor-manager.

On May 31, 1906, England was shocked to learn that a British princess, Ena Victoria, a niece of King Edward
had narrowly escaped death by an assassin's hand on her wedding day. As she and her royal husband, Alphonso X
of Spain (the two are inset) were driving in state through Madrid, a bomb was thrown which struck their carri

Photo : Topical

ey escaped unscathed, but the Queen's wedding dress was stained with the blood of victims of the attempted outrage.
e British troops acting as bodyguard to the Queen did much to stem the panic which seemed likely to spread
oughout the city.   This was by no means the first attempt which had been made upon the life of the Spanish King.

Photo : Stephen Cribb

The heir to the throne, himself a sailor, was a strong believer in a naval education. The picture shows his eldest son, who in 1907 was entered as a cadet at Osborne, being taken to the college. Two years later he proceeded to Dartmouth.

Photo : Walter Scott

Osborne House, which is in the Isle of Wight, one mile from East Cowes, was built by Queen Victoria, and presented by Edward VII to the nation in 1902. Osborne College, erected in the grounds, was opened in the following year for the training of Naval Cadets. The College was closed in 1924, the cadets being transferred to Dartmouth.

Photo : W. & D. Downey

After becoming Prince of Wales in 1901, the future King showed an increasing interest in social welfare, and particularly in the housing of the poor. In 1909, shortly after this photograph was taken, he expressed the wish that his tenants of the Duchy of Cornwall should regard him " as your friend first and your landlord afterwards."

Photo : Topical

The friendship between Great Britain and France, largely the result of Edward VII's visit to Paris in 1903, was enhanced by the Franco-British Exhibition in 1908, which was visited by King Edward and President Fallières (left).

Photo : Topical

The exhibition was held at Shepherd's Bush, London, in a gigantic " White City " specially built for the occasion. In addition to the exhibition proper a huge amusement fair was erected, a popular feature being the " Flip-flap " shown in the background, in the cars of which visitors were lifted to a great height above ground.

Photo : R. Haines

In 1906 the Liberals were returned to power with a large majority, and in 1908 David Lloyd George became Chancellor of the Exchequer.   His tenure of this important office was memorable for the introduction of far-reaching and important social reforms, including Old Age Pensions and National Health Insurance, the former in 1908, the latter in 1911.

Photo : Central Press

King Edward was a keen patron of the Turf, and maintained a large stud of fine horses. Accompanied by the Prince of Wales he visited Epsom in 1909, when his horse Minoru won the Derby, His Majesty's last classic victory.

Photo : Sport & General

No monarch ever laboured to understand the daily life of the common people as did George V. Before he became King he made numerous visits to industrial centres. Here he is seen returning from a descent into a tin mine.

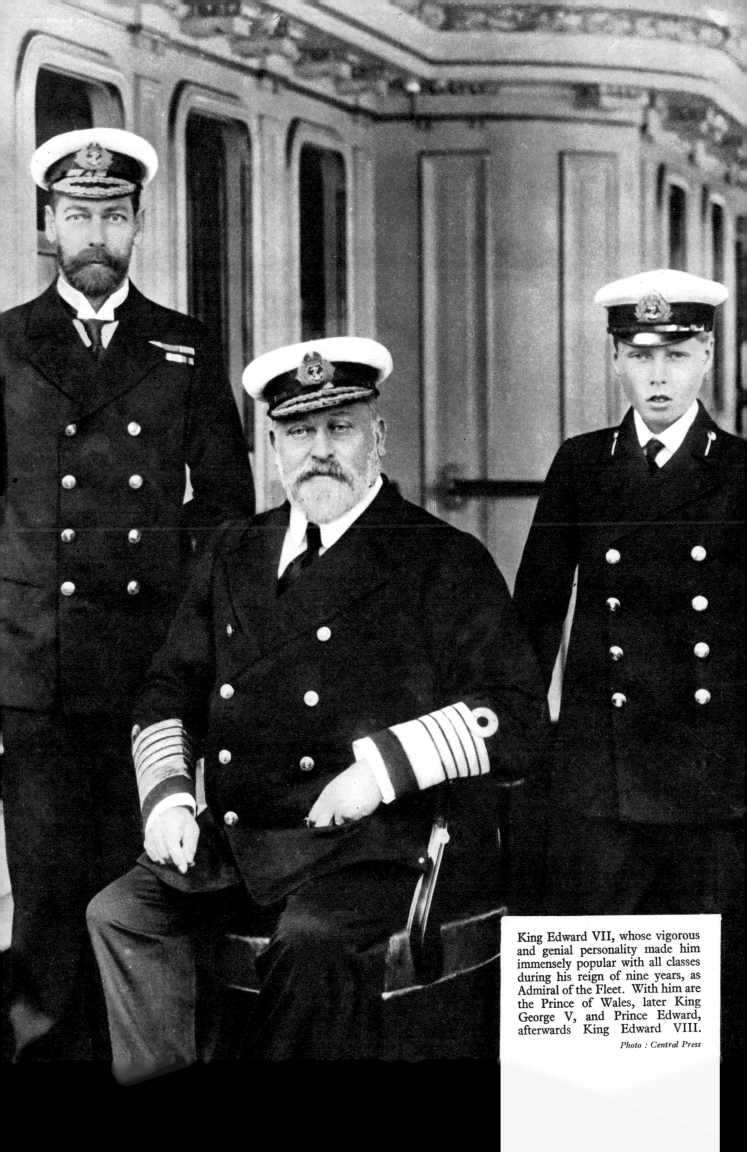

King Edward VII, whose vigorous and genial personality made him immensely popular with all classes during his reign of nine years, as Admiral of the Fleet. With him are the Prince of Wales, later King George V, and Prince Edward, afterwards King Edward VIII.

Photo : Central Press

A very brief illness ended the life of Edward VII, who passed away on May 6, 1910, at the age of 69. The King's body lay in state in the Throne Room at Buckingham Palace until May 17. Then it was conveyed to Westminster Hall, where in three days over 500,000 persons filed past the catafalque.

Photos : Topical

Nine kings followed the body of Edward VII. King George V was accompanied by the German Emperor, and after them came the Kings of Greece, Denmark, Norway, Spain, Portugal, the Belgians, and Bulgaria. Many people were deeply impressed to see in the procession the late King's charger and his favourite dog Caesar.

They buried the King in St. George's Chapel, Windsor. Memorable scenes marked the interment, showing the love felt for the late monarch by his intimate friends.

Photo : Horace W. Nicholls

Photo : Topical

The scene at Temple Bar on May 9, 1910, the day George V was proclaimed King.   According to ancient right the heralds had to obtain the Lord Mayor's permission before they could enter the City of London for the purpose, for within his City the Lord Mayor is sovereign and can forbid whom he will to enter, not even excepting his King.

King George and Queen Mary visiting in 1910 the patients of the London Hospital. With them is Princess Mary, later the Princess Royal, who was then a girl of thirteen years

Photo : Sport & General

On October 20, 1910, was launched the White Star liner *Olympic*, a ship which marked a notable advance in ocean transport. She was over 882 feet in length, and 46,000 tons gross tonnage. Her sister ship was the *Titanic*

Photo : Fox

Police and troops were rushed to Stepney on January 3, 1911, to dislodge murderers who had barricaded themselves in a house (inset) in Sidney Street. For nearly seven hours shots were exchanged. Finally the house caught fire, and when the police entered its occupants were all dead. Mr. Winston Churchill, then Home Secretary, was present.

Photos : Central Press

Photo : *Central Press*

The memorial to Queen Victoria, which stands in front of Buckingham Palace, was unveiled by King George on May 16, 1911. Standing next to him is the German Emperor, Wilhelm II, who was a grandson of the late Queen. Designed by Sir.Thomas Brock, R.A., the memorial is 82 feet high, the actual figure of Queen Victoria being 13 feet high.

King George and Queen Mary wearing the robes and insignia of the Most Noble Order of the Garter. The King is Sovereign of this highest and most ancient Order of knighthood in Great Britain, which dates back certainly to Edward III, and possibly to Richard I. The motto of the Order is " Honi soit qui mal y pense."

Photo : Topical

People began to take up positions the night before to view the coronation procession of King George V, and by 2 a.m. of June 22, 1911, Whitehall and Trafalgar Square were thronged. The royal coach (inset), drawn by light cream-coloured horses, left Buckingham Palace to the sound of artillery salutes and the strains of the National Anthem.

Photo : Central Press

Having placed the crown on the King's head, the Archbishop of Canterbury said, " God crown you with a crown of glory and righteousness, that by the ministry of this our benediction, having a right faith and manifold fruit of good works, you may obtain the crown of an everlasting kingdom by the gift of Him whose Kingdom endureth for ever."

Photo : *Sport & General and Fox*

July 13, 1911, Prince Edward, Heir-Apparent to the Throne, was at Carnarvon Castle " made and created " Prince of Wales and Earl of Chester, a dignity, dating from 1301, none but the King's eldest son may hold.   After the ceremony the Prince was led by his father and mother to the balcony, where the King presented him to his people of Wales.

The same year that he was crowned, King George left with Queen Mary to announce his accession to his Indian subjects in a magnificent Durbar at Delhi. At Port Sudan on the Red Sea he was received by Lord Kitchener.

Photo : Central Press

The Imperial procession during the state entry into Delhi on December 7, 1911. This was the first occasion in history on which the British monarch had come in person to India to be received as Emperor by his Indian subjects. Five days later the Coronation Durbar was held in the presence of over 100,000 people, amid great pomp and dignity.

Photo : Central Press

Display and pageantry signify majesty to the Oriental mind, and no ceremony exceeds in magnificence a Royal Durbar. Clad in robes of state, their crowns upon their heads, the King-Emperor and the Queen-Empress sat at Delhi on December 12, 1911, upon a lofty dais beneath a golden dome while the heralds proclaimed their coronation.

Photo : Central Press

After the Durbar and its attendant ceremonies King George spent a brief holiday in the independent state of Nepal, where he was taken tiger-hunting. On his departure from India he asserted that " We carry away lasting memories of experiences made pleasant by every means that thoughtful care and affectionate regard could devise."

Photo : Herbert G. Ponting

On June 1, 1910, the *Terra Nova* set sail from London for the Antarctic regions. Nearly three years later, on February 10, 1913, the tragic news reached England that Captain R. F. Scott, leader of the expedition, with four companions had perished after reaching the South Pole and finding the Norwegian flag already there.

" A VERY GALLANT GENTLEMAN "

" These rough notes and our dead bodies must tell the tale," wrote Captain Scott (centre) in his diary. Here are the members of the party which reached the South Pole on January 18, 1912—Scott, Wilson, Oates, Bowers and Evans.

By permission of Thos. Forman & Sons, Ltd., Nottingham

Captain Lawrence E. G. Oates, who, knowing his frostbitten condition would hinder his companions, walked from the tent to certain death in a raging blizzard, saying, " I am just going outside and I may be some time." This happened on March 17, 1912. He was never seen again, but he is always remembered as " a very gallant gentleman."

Drawn by Henry Reuterdahl.   *By courtesy of "The Illustrated London News"*

On her maiden voyage in April, 1912, the White Star liner *Titanic*, which many believed unsinkable, struck an iceberg near Cape Race just before midnight and foundered within a few hours. Of 2,224 persons on board only 735 were saved. The *Carpathia* raced to the position, which she reached at daybreak, to find wreckage and boats only.

Photo : Sport & General

In London anxious crowds of relatives gathered round the steamship offices to await the lists of survivors which were published as received. Later it was learned that the heroism of crew and passengers alike had enabled many of the women and children to be saved. Captain Smith, whose coolness did much to prevent panic, perished with his ship.

ALEXANDRA ROSE DAY

Photo : Central Press

The fiftieth anniversary of the landing of Queen Alexandra in England was celebrated by the selling of artificial roses—symbolic of the Queen's favourite flower—in the streets in aid of the hospitals. The idea caught the public imagination, and " Alexandra Rose Day " has become a national institution. The roses are made by the blind and crippled.

Photo : Horace W. Nicholls

The Royal barge, rowed by red-liveried watermen, bearing King George, Queen Mary, and Princess Mary down the regatta course at Henley on July 6, 1912, while thousands of oars were raised in salute. This was the only occasion in which King George attended this famous Regatta, which attracts the finest oarsmen from all over the world.

Photo : Topical

The Cunard liner *Aquitania*, which when launched at Glasgow in April, 1913, was the largest liner ever built in Great Britain and the world's largest ship. She was 901 feet long, with a gross tonnage of 47,000, and had a speed of 23 knots.

Photo : Sport & General

H.M.S. *Queen Elizabeth*, launched at Portsmouth on October 16, 1913, and placed on the active list of the fleet in December, 1914. On this historic battleship the surrender of the German fleet was arranged in November, 1918.

Photo : Sport & General

King George went to Berlin in May, 1913, to attend the wedding of the Kaiser's only daughter, Princess Victoria Luise, to Prince Ernst August, son of the Duke of Cumberland. King and Kaiser riding to the Potsdam review ground.

Photos : Fox and London News Agency

The years 1910 to 1914 were marked by the efforts of the militant Suffragettes to obtain votes for women by methods of violence. When arrested suffragettes fought the police, and when committed to prison they refused to eat.

Photo : Sport & General

Led by Mrs. Pankhurst, the Suffragettes broke shop windows, burnt houses and churches, raided the British Museum and exploded a bomb in Westminster Abbey. In June, 1913, a Miss Davison threw herself before the King's horse at the Derby and died later from her injuries. Not all supporters of women's suffrage approved militant methods.

Huge bell skirts, balloon sleeves, and high plumed bonnets—as shown in the top left picture—came in with the new century and were later modified into the tailored line of the lower right photograph. Skirts, however, still trailed on the ground. Above, to the right, is an evening " confection " of 1900. Below, to the left, is a view of the Row in 1902.

A " classic " line for evening wear (lower left) was fashionable concurrently with the fancy tailoring of the top left and lower right pictures till just before the War. In the upper right-hand corner is a contemporary hat and a lady cyclist of 1900 wearing bloomers. This was the forerunner of women's sports-costumes as we know them to-day.

In 1912 the variety stage was honoured by the King with its first Royal Command Performance. This took place at the Palace Theatre, Shaftesbury Avenue, W., and concluded with a grand ensemble called "Variety's Garden Party," in which the above cast of **142 artists**, most of them stars of the first rank, took part.

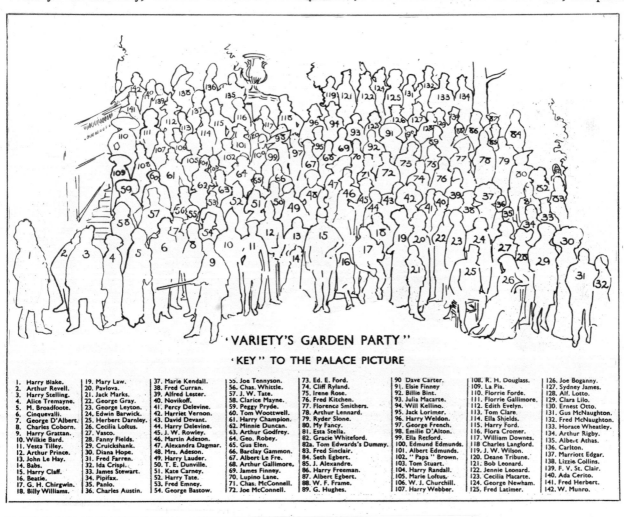

"VARIETY'S GARDEN PARTY"

"KEY" TO THE PALACE PICTURE

1. Harry Blake.
2. Arthur Revell.
3. Harry Stelling.
4. Alice Tremayne.
5. M. Broadfoote.
6. Cinquevalli.
7. George D'Albert.
8. Charles Coborn.
9. Harry Grattan.
10. Wilkie Bard.
11. Vesta Tilley.
12. Arthur Prince.
13. John Le Hay.
14. Babs.
15. Harry Claff.
16. Beatie.
17. G. H. Chirgwin.
18. Billy Williams.
19. Mary Law.
20. Pavlova.
21. Jack Marks.
22. George Gray.
23. George Leyton.
24. Edwin Barwick.
25. Herbert Darnley.
26. Cecilia Loftus.
27. Vasco.
28. Fanny Fields.
29. Cruickshank.
30. Diana Hope.
31. Fred Farren.
32. Ida Crispi.
33. James Stewart.
34. Pipifax.
35. Panlo.
36. Charles Austin.
37. Marie Kendall.
38. Fred Curran.
39. Alfred Lester.
40. Novikoff.
41. Percy Delevine.
42. Harriet Vernon.
43. David Devant.
44. Harry Delevine.
45. J. W. Rowley.
46. Martin Adeson.
47. Alexandra Dagmar.
48. Mrs. Adeson.
49. Harry Lauder.
50. T. E. Dunville.
51. Kate Carney.
52. Harry Tate.
53. Fred Emney.
54. George Bastow.
55. Joe Tennyson.
56. Chas. Whittle.
57. J. W. Tate.
58. Clarice Mayne.
59. Peggy Pryde.
60. Tom Woottwell.
61. Harry Champion.
62. Minnie Duncan.
63. Arthur Godfrey.
64. Geo. Robey.
65. Gus Elen.
66. Barclay Gammon.
67. Albert Le Fre.
68. Arthur Gallimore.
69. James Finney.
70. Lupino Lane.
71. Chas. McConnell.
72. Joe McConnell.
73. Ed. E. Ford.
74. Cliff Ryland.
75. Irene Rose.
76. Fred Kitchen.
77. Florence Smithers.
78. Arthur Lennard.
79. Ryder Slone.
80. My Fancy.
81. Esta Stella.
82. Gracie Whiteford.
82a. Tom Edwards's Dummy.
83. Fred Sinclair.
84. Seth Egbert.
85. J. Alexandre.
86. Harry Freeman.
87. Albert Egbert.
88. W. F. Frame.
89. G. Hughes.
90. Dave Carter.
91. Elsie Finney.
92. Billie Bint.
93. Julia Macarte.
94. Will Kellino.
95. Jack Lorimer.
96. Harry Weldon.
97. George French.
98. Emilie D'Alton.
99. Ella Retford.
100. Edmund Edmunds.
101. Albert Edmunds.
102. "Papa" Brown.
103. Tom Stuart.
104. Harry Randall.
105. Marie Loftus.
106. W. J. Churchill.
107. Harry Webber.
108. R. H. Douglass.
109. La Pia.
110. Florrie Forde.
111. Florrie Gallimore.
112. Edith Evelyn.
113. Tom Clare.
114. Ella Shields.
115. Harry Ford.
116. Flora Cromer.
117. William Downes.
118. Charles Langford.
119. J. W. Wilson.
120. Deane Tribune.
121. Bob Leonard.
122. Jennie Leonard.
123. Cecilia Macarte.
124. George Newham.
125. Fred Latimer.
126. Joe Boganny.
127. Sydney James.
128. Alf. Lotto.
129. Clara Lilo.
130. Ernest Otto.
131. Gus McNaughton.
132. Fred McNaughton.
133. Horace Wheatley.
134. Arthur Rigby.
135. Albert Athas.
136. Carlton.
137. Marriott Edgar.
138. Lizzie Collins.
139. F. V. St. Clair.
140. Ada Cerito.
141. Fred Herbert.
142. W. Munro.

(1) Mrs. Lambert Chambers, Women's Singles Lawn Tennis Champion at Wimbledon in 1910, 1911, 1913, and 1914; (2) A. F. Wilding, Men's Singles Lawn Tennis Champion at Wimbledon, 1910–13; (3) Tommy Burns, Heavyweight Boxing Champion of the World, 1906–8; (4) Jimmy Braid and (5) H. Vardon, who shared the golfing honours (British Open Golf Championship) with J. H. Taylor between 1900 and 1914.   In (6) the late King George V is seen talking to C. B. Fry and J. W. H. T. Douglas, two of the outstanding cricketers of the century, during a visit to Lord's in 1914.   Edward VIII (then Prince of Wales) and the Duke of York (then Prince Albert) were also present.

All forms of sport enjoyed increased popularity in the new century. New champions appeared and new records were made. Above : (1) Danny Maher, leading jockey of his day and three times winner of the Derby; (2) Vivian Woodward, the great amateur footballer who played for the Corinthians and Chelsea; (3) Sir Thomas Lipton, who built five yachts each named *Shamrock* in attempts to bring the America Cup back to this country; (4) Jimmy Wilde, Flyweight Champion of the World and outstanding British boxer of the period ; (5) Steve Bloomer (Derby County), one of the greatest footballers of the period.   Underneath (6) a typical scene at Epsom on Derby Day.

Photos 1, 2, 3 by courtesy of The Autocar, and 6 by courtesy of Humber Ltd.

During the early years of the new century rapid strides were made in the production of a reliable petrol engine, and the motor industry was soon well on its feet. (1) A 6½-h.p. Gladiator of 1901; (2) a 6-h.p. De Dion motor-car of 1904; (3) a 1904 Packard; and (6) a Humber landaulette, which represented the pinnacle of automobile design in 1907 (5) The familiar "growler" and (4) "hansom" cab were soon to disappear completely from the streets.

The petrol engine and electricity caused a revolution in transport. We illustrate above the contrasts which could be seen in the streets during this period : (1) an old horse bus and (2) a Vanguard motor bus of 1908; (4) the opening of the Clapham–Tooting Electric Tramway in 1903 by the Prince of Wales (later King George V), and (5) a horse tram on the London–Rotherhithe route, which was not closed until 1915. Petrol also made the aeroplane possible. (3) The Wright Brothers in flight and inset (A) Orville Wright and (B) Wilbur Wright, the two pioneers of air travel.

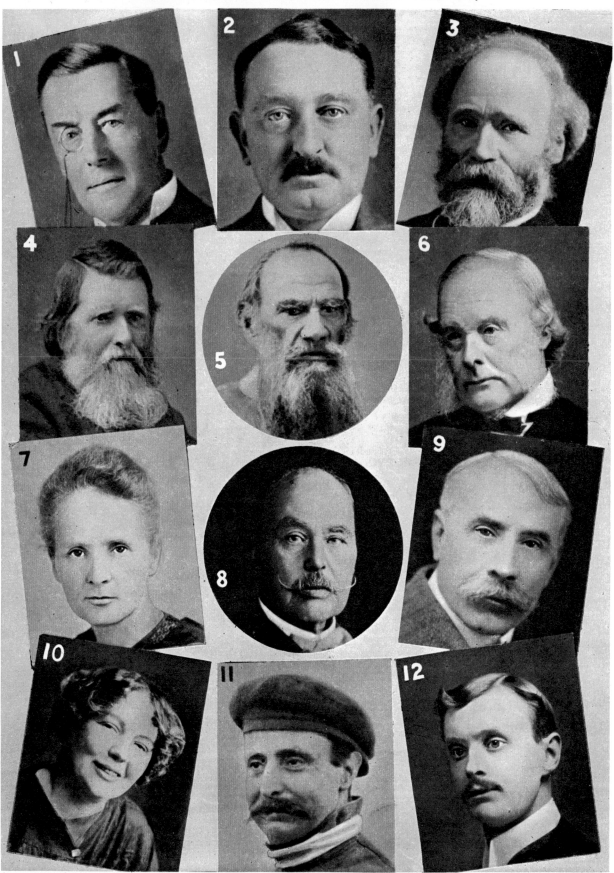

(1) Joseph Chamberlain, leader of the Tariff Reform Movement; (2) Cecil Rhodes, South African Empire Builder; (3) James Keir Hardie, Labour leader and founder of the I.L.P.; (4) John Ruskin, author of works on art and social reform; (5) Count Leo Tolstoi, Russian philosopher and novelist; (6) Lord Lister, founder of anti-septic surgery; (7) Madame Curie, who, with her brother, discovered radium; (8) Sir Ronald Ross, physician and discoverer of the transmission of malaria; (9) Sir Edward Elgar, English composer; (10) Christabel Pankhurst, leader of the suffragettes; (11) Louis Blériot, who first flew the Channel; (12) The Hon. C. S. Rolls, pioneer of the motor industry.

Photo : Wide World

The causes of the World War were many and intricate. Chief among them was the rapid rise of the German Empire, following the Franco-Prussian War. It was welded on a policy of " blood and iron " by Prince Bismarck, who from 1862 to 1890 dominated European politics. Part of a statue which ably represents his grim character is shown

Photos : Cossira

The spark that lit the flames of war was the assassination on June 28, 1914, at Serajevo, in Serbia, of the Archduke Franz Ferdinand, Heir-Presumptive to the Austro-Hungarian throne, and his wife. It took place shortly after this photograph was taken. Austria-Hungary, backed by Germany, presented an ultimatum to Serbia; Russia mobilised to protect Serbia; Germany armed, and France stood ready to help Russia. Inset are Prinzip and his victims.

Photo : E.N.A.

The actual scene of the murder of the Archduke Franz Ferdinand and his wife is marked by the man on the extreme left. The Archduke's car was reversing out of a narrow street which leads to the quays opposite the bridge when the fatal shots were fired. An earlier attempt at assassination had already been made in the suburbs.

Great Britain strove to the last to preserve peace, but the violation of Belgian neutrality by German troops led to the sending of an ultimatum to Germany. On the night of August 4, 1914, vast crowds waited anxiously in London, but no reply was received. At 12.15 a.m. on August 5 it was officially announced that a state of war existed.

Photo : Fox

The neutrality of Belgium was guaranteed by the Treaty of London signed in 1831 by Great Britain, Austria, France, Prussia and Russia. Britain respected this treaty: the German Chancellor, Bethmann von Hollweg, retorted that "just for a scrap of paper Great Britain was going to make war on a kindred nation who desired nothing better than to be friends with her." Inset: The Kaiser, von Hollweg, Sir Edward Grey, and Albert, King of the Belgians.

(1) Rt. Hon. Winston Churchill; (2) Rt. Hon. H. H. Asquith, Prime Minister; (3) Lord Fisher; (4) General Joffre; (5) Sir John French; (6) Sir John Jellicoe; (7) Admiral von Tirpitz; (8) General von Hindenburg; (9) General Ludendorff; (10) General von Kluck; (11) Lord Kitchener, Secretary for War; (12) General von Moltke.

On August 17, 1914, the British Press Bureau reported that "The Expeditionary Force, as detailed for foreign service, has been safely landed on French soil. The embarkation, transportation and disembarkation of men and stores were alike carried through with the greatest possible precision and without a single casualty." The force consisted of 50,000 infantry with its artillery and five cavalry brigades. Above: leaving England; below, arriving at Boulogne.

Photos : I.W.M.

The sack of Louvain in Belgium by the Germans on August 26, 1914, shocked public opinion everywhere. The cathedral of St. Pierre, the magnificent university library containing thousands of priceless books and manuscripts, and 1,120 houses were destroyed when the Germans set fire to the city, and seventy-nine persons were shot.

Meanwhile, in Belgium, in northern France, and in half a dozen other European countries thousands upon thousands of homeless refugees fled from the ghastly terrors of modern warfare. Perhaps the most heartrending scenes were those in Serbia during the following year, when powerful Austro-German armies overran the country.

KITCHENER'S ARMIES

"*YOUR King and Country need you*" was the slogan which called hundreds of thousands of eager recruits to the Colours in 1914 and early 1915. Under the direction of Lord Kitchener these men were grouped into "new armies" and underwent training for active service. The military depots and areas were quite inadequate, so that men drilling in parks and other open spaces became familiar sights in all parts of the country.

Photos : Sport & General : Topical

"YOUR COUNTRY NEEDS **YOU**"

When the Expeditionary Force left, King George wrote: "I shall follow your every movement with deepest interest." In November, 1914, he crossed to France and spent several days with his troops, making an extensive tour of the battle area. He is here seen with Sir Douglas Haig, commander of the 1st Army Corps, decorating a soldier.

Photo : Central Press.

One of the minor naval engagements of the war took place on Jan. 24, 1915, at the Dogger Bank, when the German armoured cruiser *Blucher* was sunk. Vice-Admiral Sir David Beatty on the *Lion* was in command of the British forces.

Photo : L.N.A.

Painted by Cyrus Cuneo

The attempt to force the Dardanelles was begun in February, 1915, when British and French battleships bombarded the forts at the entrance. In April, British, Australian and Indian troops stormed heights on the Gallipoli peninsula.

Photo : I.W.M.

For nearly twelve months the Allies maintained a precarious hold, but Gallipoli proved impregnable, and was evacuated in January, 1916. The only casualties sustained were one man killed and one wounded during the evacuation, which was carried out by Generals Birdwood and Davies with the assistance of Admiral de Robeck.

The Cunard liner *Lusitania* was torpedoed by a German submarine off the south coast of Ireland on May 7, 1915, and sank within half an hour. Of 1,906 persons on board, only 708 were saved. The ruthless destruction of non-combatants did much to bring the United States into the war.

Anxious men and women who had relatives and friends on board the *Lusitania* streamed into the offices of the Cunard Steamship Company. As boats with survivors arrived their names were telegraphed to England.

Photo: Topical

Photo : I.W.M

Directly war broke out the Prince of Wales begged to be allowed to go to France, and before the end of 1914 he got his way. A prominent Labour leader of the time has told how the Prince " caused his military superiors not a little anxiety by reason of the personal risks he ran from time to time." It is said he once took part in an attack.

Photo : Topical

Miss Edith Cavell, who while head of a training school for nurses in Brussels during the German occupation, enabled many British, French and Belgian soldiers to escape from Belgium. She was shot by the Germans on October 12, 1915. Her last words were : " I realise that patriotism is not enough. I must have no hatred or bitterness towards anyone." An impressive memorial (seen above) is erected to her memory and stands at the bottom of St. Martin's Lane, London.

THE BATTLE OF JUTLAND

Photos : I.W.M.

The hard-fought battle of Jutland between the British and German fleets took place on May 31 and June 1, 1916. Vice-Admiral Sir David Beatty bore the brunt of the opening phase of the conflict. The German High Sea Fleet escaped in a badly mauled condition and never again contested the British command of the sea, despite the fact that 6,274 British officers and men were killed or taken prisoners as against the enemy's 2,545, and fourteen British vessels were sunk. The top photograph shows the German battle-cruiser *Seydlitz* heavily engaged. Below, the *Queen Mary* going down in clouds of smoke and steam shortly after the battle opened, and Vice-Admiral Sir David Beatty.

Photo : Daily Express.

Lord Kitchener on H.M.S. *Iron Duke* just before going on board H.M.S. *Hampshire*. He was proceeding on an important mission to Russia. When west of the Orkney Isles the ship was torpedoed or mined, and sank with all hands on June 5, 1916. Prolonged search by patrol vessels revealed only a capsized boat and some bodies.

Photo : I.W.M.

During the early months of the war the British force suffered greatly through shortage of ammunition. A tremendous drive by Mr. Lloyd George as Minister of Munitions put matters right, and from mid-1916 the guns were kept well supplied. For the remainder of the war the British were superior in artillery on the Western Front.

Photo : I.W.M.

On July 1, 1916, after an intensive bombardment, the British armies launched a series of gigantic attacks on the Somme which persisted until November. Troops advanced to the attack over ground pulverised by artillery. Spades were carried, for trenches were everywhere wrecked and battered, and fresh ones had to be dug after every attack.

Photo : I.W.M

During the battles of the Somme troops which had taken part in an attack were withdrawn from the front line as soon as possible and kept in reserve for counter-attacks. They usually " rested " in abandoned trenches, being employed as working parties, digging defensive works or carrying supplies and ammunition to men in the front line.

Photo : Central Press

Bombing raids by enemy aircraft brought the terrors of war to civilians remote from the battle area. London suffered severely on several occasions between 1915 and 1918. The above shows damage done in the first raid on London.

Photo : Topical

Other victims of frightfulness. In spite of elaborate defensive measures, no fewer than 103 raids took place in which 8,578 bombs were dropped, killing 1,414 people and wounding 3,416. Streets remained unlighted, and it was a penal offence to show a light after nightfall. Maroons and placards warned people of impending attack.

Photo : I.W.M.

British Dominions and Colonies responded magnificently to the call of the Motherland during the World War. The Canadians won undying fame during the second battle of Ypres, when they were the first British troops to meet a gas attack, and later during the battles of the Somme, on Vimy Ridge, and at the taking of Passchendaele.

Photo : I.W.M.

The Anzacs (Australians and New Zealanders), heroes of the Gallipoli landings, later saw service in France, Palestine, and Syria. The gallantry of the South Africans at Delville Wood on the Somme is ever memorable, as is that of the Newfoundlanders at Monchyle Preux. Troops from the Indian Empire served on almost every front.

Photo : I.W.M.

Aeroplanes played an important part on all fronts. Airmen observed movements and concentrations of the enemy, " spotted " for the artillery, bombed ammunition dumps and store depots, and made photographs of the trenches and dispositions of the foe. Aerial combats were frequent during a continuous struggle for mastery of the air.

Photo : I.W.M.

Poison gas was first used by the Germans in April, 1915, and later became a regular offensive weapon on both sides. It was either released from cylinders in a dense cloud on to the enemy trenches, or fired in shells that burst on impact. Chlorine was the first gas used, and later the dreaded mustard gas. Inset: soldiers with gas-masks.

Photo : I.W.M.

On the Western Front men fought and died on ground " rendered almost impassable by overflowing brooks and deep shell-holes and a general covering of liquid mud, ground every yard of which had to be gained in face of intense bombardments, incessant machine-gun fire, and continual and determined counter-attacks by the enemy.

Photo : I.W.M.

Meanwhile in Mesopotamia and Palestine and on other eastern fronts troops marched hundreds of miles across torrid deserts and stony wastes where often the heat was so great that the steel of their rifles burnt their hands, while to remove a sun helmet from the head for more than an instant was to court death by sunstroke.

Photo : Central Press

While the men went to the war, women did their work. They became sweeps, coal-heavers, and navvies, railway porters, taxi-drivers, and 'bus conductors, agricultural labourers and gardeners, bill-posters, electricians, street-cleaners, shop assistants, and clerks. There were very few occupations in which women did not play a prominent part.

Photo : L.N.A.

By January, 1917, nearly four and a half million British women were engaged in commerce and industry, not counting another two million domestic servants, charwomen, and occasional helps. Of these over a million were war workers taking the place of men. Scores of thousands were engaged in the munition factories throughout the country.

Photo : I.W.M.

The canteens provided behind the fighting line by the Y.M.C.A. and other organisations were godsends to troops resting between spells in the trenches.   Here English cigarettes and tobacco, and " dry " goods could be obtained, and often the luxury of a cooked meal.   Rooms were often provided for reading and writing, and concerts were given.

Photo : I.W.M.

When a soldier was wounded he was treated first at an advanced dressing post, then sent to a casualty clearing station, from which the hospital train and ship bore the " lucky ones " back to " blighty "—as England was universally called in those days.   A wound which earned the return of a soldier to the Motherland was also called a " blighty."

Photos : Cossira and Wide World.

Discontent, fostered by incompetency and corruption, military disasters, and food shortage, brought about a revolution in Russia in March, 1917. The Czar abdicated and a moderate Socialist republic under Alexander Kerensky was set up which launched a disastrous offensive against Austria in July. Kerensky lost his hold upon the masses, and between October 26 and November 7 the Bolsheviks, headed by Trotsky, but with Lenin as the master mind, seized power with the declared intention of offering "an immediate democratic peace." By the end of November the Soviet government held sway throughout the country, and Russia made peace with the Central Powers at Brest-Litovsk in March, 1918. Lenin (inset) died in 1924. His embalmed body lies in a granite tomb in Moscow, which is also shown.

Photo : I.W.M.

On December 9, 1917, following the capture of Beersheba and Gaza, Jerusalem was surrendered to General Sir.
Edmund Allenby by the mayor. Two days later the General entered the Holy City on foot. Before succeeding
Sir Archibald Murray, the General had been in command of the British Third Army on the Western Front.

Photos : I.W.M. and Central Press

During 1917 and 1918 the Navy was mainly engaged in com-
bating the German submarine menace, which at one period
proved a serious threat to the transport and ships of the Allies.
King George, seen here mounting from a British submarine to
a battleship, warmly commended the vigilance and initiative with
which the U-boats, although they secured many victims, were
relentlessly hunted down. Bombed by aircraft, shot at by guns,
rammed when opportunity served and chased by destroyers
which dropped explosive depth charges, every moment of the
lives of commanders and crews was fraught with anxiety.
Although over 5,400 vessels were sunk by enemy submarines,
203 of the latter perished before the conflict came to an end.

Photo : I.W.M.

During the spring of 1917 the German forces on the Western Front voluntarily retired from the positions in the Somme area, which they had defended with such stubborness in 1916, to the famous Hindenburg line, an intricate system of heavily fortified trenches between the Vimy Ridge on the north and the Chemin des James ridge in the south.

Photo : I.W.M.

The British armies advanced to occupy the evacuated positions. Here Australian troops are seen marching into Bapaume, which for long has lain just beyond the German lines. The remainder of the year was devoted to a series of powerful but costly attacks, in which the Vimy Ridge, Messines, and Passchendaele were captured.

Photo : I.W.M.

British staff officers in a typical dug-out on the Western Front. These dug-outs were built beneath the trenches, from six to twenty feet below ground. Their accommodation included rough tables and seats, with wire netting or sack beds. German dug-outs were usually bigger, frequently deeper, and sometimes lit by electric light.

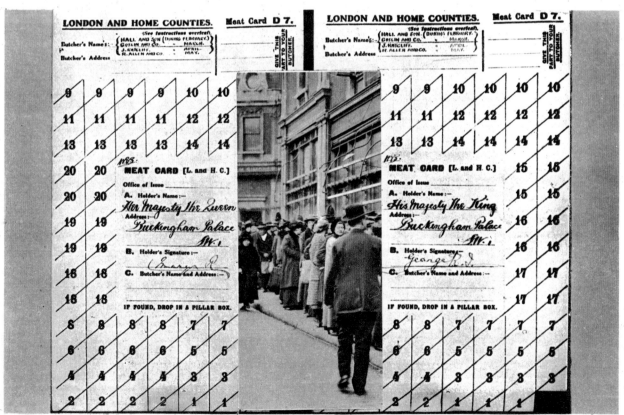

Photo : Sport & General

In Britain rationing of food began in 1917, and continued with increasing severity throughout that year and the next. Like their subjects, the King and Queen had ration cards. So short were supplies that people often queued up for hours to buy food, and closed butchers' shops bearing the notice " No Meat " were by no means unusual.

Photo : I.W.M.

ON March 21, 1918, the Germans launched their last and greatest attack on the Western front. The brunt of it fell upon the British Fifth Army, which was holding a very extended line with depleted forces. The Germans broke through on a wide front and for weeks the Allies were unable to stem their advance. On April 11, Sir Douglas Haig issued a Special Order of the Day, and a facsimile of the stirring message as he originally wrote it is given below. It has been stated many times by foreign observers and also by outspoken critics of their own race that the British never realise the seriousness of a position or the possibility of disaster until it is imminent. Doubtless Sir Douglas Haig had this characteristic trait in mind when penning the stirring appeal to his badly pressed men, for it will be noted that the optimistic strain in which he concluded the letter was scratched out when he revised it for publication. " But be of good cheer, the British Empire must win in the End " did not appeal. The King crossed to France and spent several days at the Front.

Photo : I.W.M.

Photo : I.W.M.

The big German push of 1918 drove the Allied armies back to the Marne, thus compelling a greater retreat than any since September, 1914. Throughout these dark days the British Army maintained, in Haig's words, a " splendid resistance," notwithstanding that in three weeks the enemy threw 106 divisions into the battle.

Photo : I.W.M.

The attack was preceded by a bombardment from 6,000 German guns, which poured high explosive, gas and smoke shells on to the British lines. In fifteen days Haig's armies lost 90,000 prisoners and 1,200 guns and had retreated thirty-eight miles, while immense quantities of munitions and stores were smashed by artillery or lay derelict.

Photo : I.W.M.

By a daring exploit carried out on April 23, 1918, the harbour of Zeebrugge in Belgium, a German U-boat base, was sealed by the sinking in the fairway of three old vessels filled with concrete. A cutting-out expedition from H.M.S. *Vindictive* wrecked gun emplacements, and the jetty connecting the Mole with the mainland was destroyed.

Photo: I.W.M.

The Zeebrugge raid was carried out under the command of Vice-Admiral Roger Keyes. The men chosen to man the block-ships and for the storming and demolition parties were all volunteers from the Royal Navy (part of which is seen here at Rosyth) and the Royal Marines. Only a small proportion of the men who volunteered could be used.

Photo : Central Press

" This anniversary," said the King, in a sympathetic message on July 6, 1918, " falls at a time when the shadow of war lies heavily on our land, and the very existence of the Empire is assailed by an unscrupulous foe. In this time of trial it is our earnest desire to share the sorrows of our people, and, so far as in us lies, to alleviate their sufferings."

Photo : I.W.M.

" Less than six months after the launching of the great German offensive which was to have cut the Allied front in two, the Allied Armies are everywhere to-day advancing victoriously side by side over the same battlefields on which by the courage and steadfastness of their defence they broke the enemy's assaults."—Sir Douglas Haig, September 10, 1918.

Mutiny at Kiel, the chief naval port, on November 3, 1918, disorders at Hamburg and Bremen, and a revolution in the capital, where the Socialists refused to support the Government, helped the fall of the tottering German Empire. Although there was fighting in the capital, the majority of the troops sided with the revolutionists.

On November 6, 1918, German delegates left Berlin to ask the Generalissimo of the Allied Forces for an armistice. The delegates were met by Allied Staff Officers, and, as the armistice had not yet been granted, were led blindfold through the Allied lines. The Kaiser signed his abdication at Spa on the 9th and fled to neutral Holland.

Photos : Sport & General and Fox

MAROONS signalled the signing of Armistice, and Great Britain, from the capital to the remotest hamlet, went wild with enthusiasm. Munition workers flocked out of the factories, employers and employees left their desks, sirens screamed and whistles sounded. While essential services were maintained those who were able to do so flocked to town halls, parks and other public centres to give vent to feelings too long pent up and made holiday. Lumber rooms were ransacked for flags and bunting, and many places were gaily decorated with paper chains and roses that had done service many years before and been almost forgotten in the dark days of the war. An enormous crowd gathered outside Buckingham Palace. Conspicuous among the thousands who cheered were nurses and wounded soldiers.

The joy of the people of London who thronged the neighbourhood of Buckingham Palace was fully shared by the King and Queen, who appeared on the historic balcony soon after 11 a.m., and were accorded an enthusiastic reception. In many parts of the metropolis traffic was forced to a standstill by densely packed throngs of people who felt that at long last a crushing burden had suddenly slipped from their shoulders.

Photo : L.N.A.

On November 21, 1918, the main portion of the German Fleet surrendered. The large vessels were met at sea by the Grand Fleet and escorted to the Firth of Forth, while the submarines proceeded to Harwich. During the morning Sir David Beatty made the historic signal : " The German flag will be hauled down at sunset to-day and will not be hoisted again without permission." The main units were afterwards taken to Scapa Flow in the Orkneys. In the following June nearly all the ships interned there were scuttled by their crews while the British battle-fleet was absent on gunnery practice. The vessels given up included ten battle-ships, six battle-cruisers, eight light cruisers, fifty destroyers, and 185 submarines. Certain German ships which did not cross the North Sea were disarmed in their home ports under the superintendence of Admiral Browning.

Photo : Fox

Hats, which had been cartwheel size, became small and military looking. Waists went high and the three-quarter-length outline with its widest point just above the knee came in and stayed. Top, left : A frilled afternoon dress of 1915. Top, right : One of the last of the big hats. Below : A waistline tailored costume worn with a dashing helmet-toque. Bottom, left : A memory of pre-bobbed hair and a " Russian " mode of 1917-18.

The top left photograph shows an evening dress whose trailing lines give place to the shorter tunic effect shown below. In the same way the somewhat slovenly costumes, like that at the top right corner, became simpler and more severe (bottom right). The top centre shows a "lampshade" type of skirt popular in the early years of the war. Below, a big hat that was to give place to close-fitting small brimmed models for the next decade.

(1) Dame Clara Butt, the celebrated contralto; (2) Oscar Asche, actor and producer; (3) Gaby Deslys, the famous French dancer; (4) Alice Delysia, French comedy actress; (5) José Collins, musical comedy star; (6) Violet Loraine, revue star; (7) Sir Harry Lauder, of music hall fame; (8) George Grossmith, comedy actor; (9) George Robey, the great comedian; (10) Charlie Chaplin and (11) Mary Pickford, film stars; (12) Rudolph Valentino, idol of the screen.

CHAMPIONS OF SPORT 1915-1925

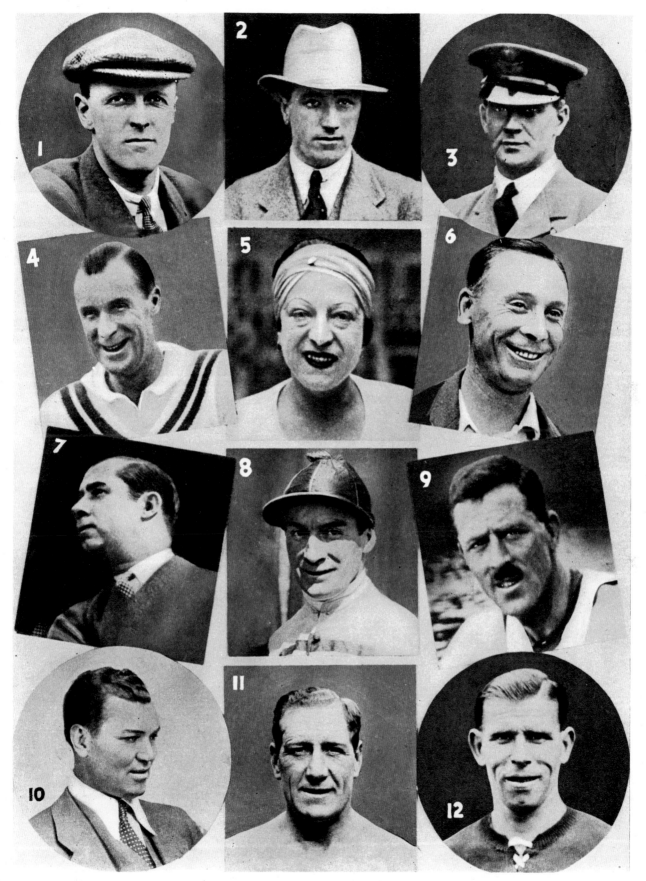

(1) Henry Segrave, racing motorist; (2) Sir John Alcock and (3) Sir A. W. Brown, the first men to fly the Atlantic; (4) W. T. Tilden and (5) Susanne Lenglen, lawn tennis champions; (6) Jack Hobbs, great cricketer; (7) Walter Hagen, American golfer; (8) Steve Donoghue, famous jockey; (9) Ernest Barry, sculling champion; (10) Jack Dempsey, boxing champion; (11) "Bombardier" Billy Wells, British boxer; (12) Charlie Buchan, international footballer.

Photos : Flight and Central Press

(1) A two-seater Bristol fighter; (2) a Handley-Page heavy bomber of 1917; (3) the machine which Sir Charles Kingsford Smith used in his first attempt to fly to Australia; (4) the machine used by Sir John Alcock and Sir A. W. Brown on the first flight ever made from America to England (1919); (5) a Handley-Page air-liner built for Imperial Airways in 1922; (6) an experiment that failed—the R.34, one of the R class airships built by the British Government.

Above are illustrated types of vehicles which made motoring so popular during this period. (1) An early type of open-topped omnibus with solid tyres; (2) an early taxi; (3) an Austin Seven of 1922—a type of motor-car which brought motoring within the range of means of the general public; (4) a B.S.A. motor-cycle of 1925, and (5) the type of open charabanc, so popular just after the war. During this period, 'motoring for the million' became a reality.

(1) Woodrow Wilson, American statesman; (2) Marshal Foch, leader of the Allied Armies; (3) Georges Clemenceau, the " Tiger," French statesman and patriot; (4) Lord Reading, Lord Chief Justice and Viceroy of India; (5) Lord Birkenhead, Lord Chancellor; (6) Lord Balfour, and (7) Mr. Bonar Law, English statesman; (8) Lord Carson, lawyer and Ulster patriot; (9) Rosita Forbes, the famous explorer; (10) Lawrence of Arabia, author, soldier and friend of the Arabs; (11) General Smuts, South African statesman; (12) Gertrude Bell, an explorer of Arabia.

(1) Dr. Robert Bridges, poet Laureate; (2) H. G. Wells, sociologist and author; (3) Thomas Hardy, the novelist of Dorsetshire; (4) John Galsworthy, dramatist and novelist; (5) Mary Webb, the famous novelist; (6) Sir William Orpen, the famous R.A.; (7) Professor Einstein, originator of the relativity theory; (8) Sir J. J. Thomson, the famous English scientist; (9) Marchese Marconi, inventor of wireless; (10) Sir Ernest Shackleton, and (11) Fridtjof Nansen, explorers of the South and North Poles; (12) Lilian Baylis, manager of the Old Vic and Sadlers Wells Theatres.

From the painting by Sir William Orpen, R.A

" Gentlemen, I leave you to your weighty deliberations, and I declare open the Conference of Paris."   Thus did the French President, M. Poincaré, inaugurate the Peace Conference at Versailles, on the afternoon of January, 18, 1919. Only the Allied and Associated Powers were present, representatives of the defeated countries being invited later when terms had been prepared.   The Conference was dominated by the " Big Four," Lloyd George, Clemenceau, President Wilson, and Signor Orlando, Italy's representative.   At the second full meeting of the Conference, President Wilson moved a resolution, which was carried, for the establishment of a League of Nations.   He argued that a league must exist to protect the common interest and to maintain peace in the world.   He said that the destiny of humanity was now in the hands of ordinary people, and that they demanded that nevermore should mankind be used as puppets in a game.   The proposal had the support of Mr. Lloyd George, Signor Orlando and M. Léon Bourgeois, a French statesman who had long advocated such a league.   The draft treaty was communicated to Germany in May.

The Treaty of Versailles was signed on June 28, 1919, and was announced throughout England by Royal Proclamation. In a message to his people that same day King George said : " I share my people's joy and thanksgiving, and earnestly pray that the coming years of peace may bring to them ever-increasing happiness and prosperity."

On July 21 the whole of Great Britain gave itself up to a day of rejoicing for Peace. The central feature of the celebrations in London was the great Victory Procession, in which all sections of the Forces took part, including the battle-scarred " Old Contemptibles " of 1914. Inset is Sir Douglas Haig, who as Commander-in-Chief, led the Procession.

Moving scenes were witnessed as the procession passed the newly-erected Cenotaph in Whitehall, simply inscribed to "The Glorious Dead." Soldiers stood on guard with arms reversed and a gentle breeze fluttered the flags. Vice-Admiral Sir David Beatty may be seen immediately behind the Union Jack in the foreground.

Photo : Central Press

Part of the huge throng of people which followed the Victory March across Westminster Bridge. Meanwhile in every city, town and village people gave rein to their feelings. Processions, sports, and open-air dancing were to be seen everywhere. At night the lights of innumerable bonfires blazed the glad tidings of peace across the sky.

Photo: L.N.A.

On November 11, 1919, the first anniversary of the Armistice, the entire British nation, in response to an invitation by King George, stood in silence for two minutes at 11 o'clock in remembrance of all who had given their lives in the War. In Whitehall immense crowds stood reverently as King George placed a wreath at the foot of the Cenotaph, a name derived from the Greek and meaning an empty tomb. The monument, designed by Sir Edwin Lutyens, R.A., was a temporary structure pending the completion of the permanent memorial, and the famous architect produced a rough sketch within a few hours of the suggestion. After the simple ceremony a vast number of people filed past the Cenotaph and deposited a forest of flowers ranging from tiny bunches to elaborate garlands.

November 11, 1920, was memorable for two deeply significant ceremonies, the unveiling by the King of the permanent Cenotaph, and the burial of the Unknown Warrior in Westminster Abbey. It is uncertain who first suggested the idea of bringing home and interring in the venerable shrine the body of a British soldier " unknown by name or rank," but once mooted it fired popular imagination to an unprecedented degree. As the gun-carriage passed the Cenotaph, King George laid on it a wreath inscribed with the words, " In proud memory of those warriors who died unknown in the Great War. Unknown, and yet well known; as dying, and behold they live. George R.I."

Photo : Central Press

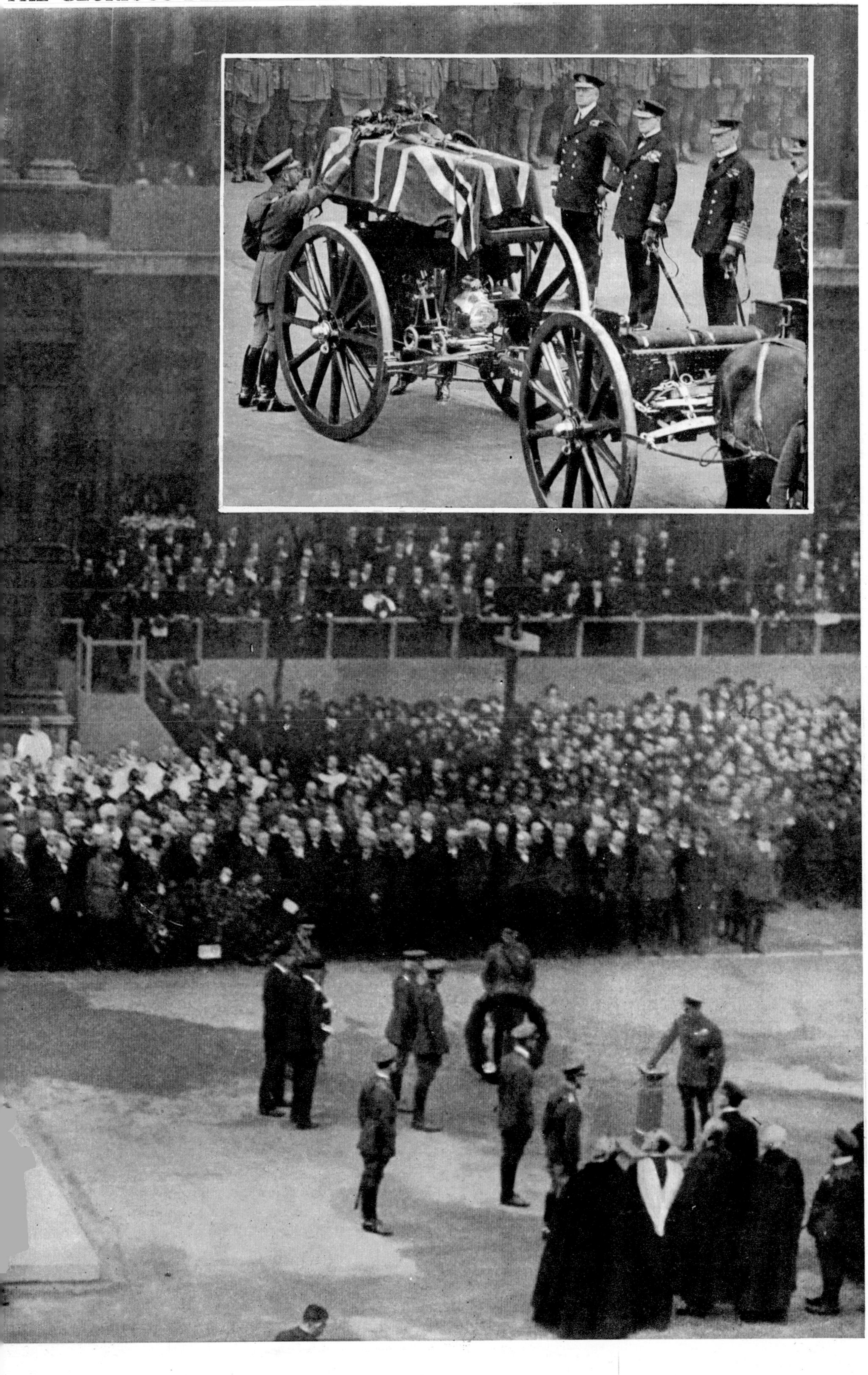

Photo : L.N.A.

Great crowds of mourners filed through the nave of Westminster Abbey to pay homage to the Unknown Warrior at his lying-in-state. A simple brass slab marks the last resting-place of the British soldier brought from France to commemorate " the many multitudes who during the Great War of 1914-1918 gave the most that man can give, life itself."

FIRST PARLIAMENT OF NORTHERN IRELAND

Photos : *Central Press*

Opening the first Parliament of Northern Ireland at the City Hall, Belfast, on June 22, 1921, King George said : "I pray that my coming to Ireland to-day may prove to be the first step towards an end of strife amongst her people . . . I appeal to all Irishmen to pause, to stretch out the hand of forbearance and conciliation, to forgive and to forget, and to join in making for the land which they love a new era of peace, contentment and goodwill." Inset : the fine New Parliament Buildings at Stormont, near Belfast, which were opened in 1932 by the Prince of Wales.

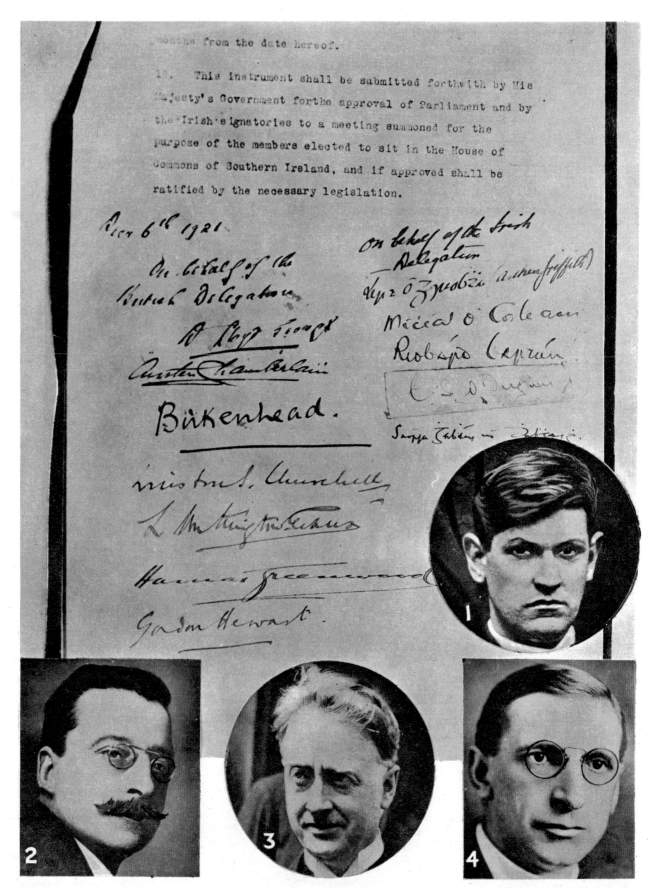

Photos : Topical

The King's appeal was not in vain. By a treaty signed December 6, 1921, by Messrs. Michael Collins (1), Arthur Griffith (2), Robert Barton, Eamoun S. Duggan, and George Gavan Duffy, southern Ireland became a British Dominion. Mr. Cosgrave (3) President of the Executive Council 1922-32; Mr. de Valera (4) opposed the treaty.

Photo : Central Press (top)

On February 28, 1922, Princess Mary, only daughter of the King and Queen, was married at Westminster Abbey to Viscount Lascelles, D.S.O., eldest son of the Earl of Harewood, the bride being in her twenty-fifth year.   After the ceremony the wedding group appeared on the balcony at Buckingham Palace to receive the ovation of a large crowd.

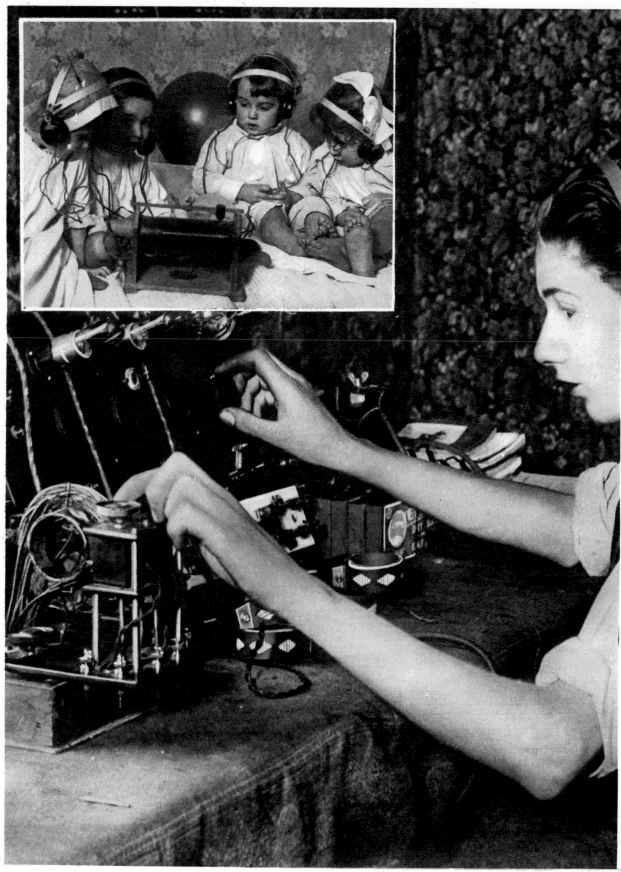

Photos : Topical and Photopress

The years 1920 to 1922 saw the advent of broadcasting. Many clever youngsters made small fortunes by building receiving sets for the thousands of people who were clamouring for them. For listening-in headphones were used, the loud-speaker being still in its noisy and disconcerting infancy, while most of the sets were crystal receivers.

Photo : Central Press

A family group taken in 1923 showing Queen Alexandra, officially styled the Queen Mother, then in her seventy-ninth year, King George, and Princess Mary, Viscountess Lascelles, with her eldest son, George Henry Hubert, born February 7, 1923. A second son, Gerald David, was born to Princess Mary on August 21 of the following year.

Photo : Bassano

Few Royal unions have been more popular than that of the Duke of York with Lady Elizabeth Angela Marguerite Bowes-Lyon, the youngest daughter of the Earl and Countess of Strathmore, which took place on April 26, 1924.

Photo : Elliott & Fry

For the first time in the annals of British history a Labour Government took office in January, 1924. Mr. Ramsay MacDonald was Premier, Mr. Philip (later Viscount) Snowden, Chancellor of the Exchequer, and Mr. Arthur Henderson, Home Secretary. From the left of the picture they occupy the fifth, third and eighth chairs respectively.

Photo : L.N.A.

" This Exhibition," said the King on April 23, 1924, " will enable us to take stock of the resources, actual and potential, of the Empire as a whole, to consider where these exist and how they can best be developed and utilised, to take counsel together how the peoples can co-operate to supply one another's needs and to promote national well-being."

Photo : L.N.A.

After the official ceremony in the Stadium a cable announcing the opening of the British Empire Exhibition circled the world in fifty-five seconds. The King and Queen made a tour of some of the many buildings, which, with the grounds surrounding them covered 220 acres and revealed " the whole Empire in little," to quote the King's words.

VICTORY OF A DERBY FAVOURITE

The King was present at the Derby of 1924, when Sansovino won the famous race by six lengths. There were twenty-seven runners and two false starts were made. Sansovino was owned by Lord Derby, trained by George Lambton, and ridden by Tommy Weston. The going was heavy and treacherous owing to continuous rain.

King George was the first British monarch to attend a Cup Final. He was present at the first final in the Wembley Stadium in 1924 when the crowd rushed the barriers, and afterwards showed his interest in football by attending every year unless the state of his health made it inadvisable. Wembley Stadium holds nearly 94,000 people.

Photo : Express Photos

People came from all over the world for the railway centenary celebrations at Darlington in July, 1925, when the whole story of railway transport was displayed in a six-miles-long procession of locomotives and trains. Above is shown " Locomotion I," built by George Stephenson for the Stockton and Darlington Railway in 1825.

Photo : L.N.A.

Among those who derived great enjoyment from the moving pageant were the Duke and Duchess of York. They watched from one of the temporary grandstands at Urlay Nook and afterwards made a closer and more intimate inspection of some of the oldest and newest locomotives by walking along the permanent way for some distance.

Photo : L.N.A.

Queen Alexandra, who died at Sandringham on November 20, 1925, was greatly beloved by all sections of the people for her charm and kindliness. Born in 1844, she came to England in 1863 as the bride of the future King Edward VII.

Photo : Central Press

To guarantee fulfilment of the terms of the Treaty of Versailles, Allied troops were to occupy Rhineland territory and bridgeheads for fifteen years. The period was shortened, and the British troops left Cologne, which was their headquarters in January, 1926. Above the Union Jack is being hauled down before the evacuation of the city.

Photos : Fox and Photopress

On March 6, 1926, the Shakespeare Memorial Theatre at Stratford-upon-Avon was destroyed by fire. The Shakespeare relics were saved.

Photo : Fox

A national fund for the erection of a new theatre was immediately started, and six years later the present stately building designed by Miss Elizabeth Scott was completed. Thoroughly modern and dignified in conception, it was opened by the Prince of Wales and dedicated by him " to the immortal memory of William Shakespeare."

Photo : Fox

The only general stoppage of work in the history of Great Britain took place in May, 1926, following the breakdown of negotiations between coal miners and owners. The other unions supported the miners, and for nine days the industrial machine was paralysed. Skeleton transport services run by amateur volunteers rarely needed official protection.

As few, if any, trains, trams, or buses were running from the suburbs, office workers in London whose employment was not affected by the stoppage had to find other means of reaching their places of business. Thousands decided to walk, and a vast army of cyclists poured into town by every road. Many of these people had not cycled for years.

Those who had private cars took all the friends they could squeeze in, while no pedestrian ever hesitated to ask for a lift from even a complete stranger. Empty lorries of every description were eagerly seized upon, and " Twopenny Tailboard Trips " soon came to rank among the most popular of all the methods employed in order to get to work.

Photo : Fox

Twice during 1926 was the North Pole crossed by aircraft, the first flight being made on May 9 by two Americans, Lieut.-Com. Richard E. Byrd and Floyd Bennett. Three days later Roald Amundsen crossed the Pole in an airship.

Photo : L.N.A.

An enthusiastic reception awaited Mr. (later Sir) Alan Cobham when on October 1, 1926, he alighted on the Thames at Westminster after a record flight to Australia and back in which he covered 26,000 miles in 320 flying hours. Afterwards the aviator was conducted up the Palace Landing Stairs and taken to the Terrace of the House.

After the King-Emperor's pronouncement at his Durbar in 1911 that Delhi was to be the capital of the Indian Empire the building of a new Imperial City and Parliament House was put in hand. In January 1927 the Viceroy of India, Lord Irwin (later Viscount Halifax) in the presence of the members of the three legislative bodies and a brilliant gathering of Indian princes, declared open the great Council House of all India (inset). The top picture shows the Secretarial buildings and the lower the Viceroy's House.

Photos : Fox and Sport & General

The Duke and Duchess of York left England early in 1927 for Australia, where on May 9 His Royal Highness opened the Parliament building at Canberra, a new city designed as the capital of the Commonwealth. "May this day's ceremony," said the Duke in his speech, "mark the rededication of this Commonwealth to those great ideals of liberty, fair dealing, justice and devotion to the cause of peace for which the Empire and all its members stand."

Photo: Sport & General

Charles Augustus (later Colonel) Lindbergh, the American aviator who, on May 20, 1927, commenced the first solo flight of the Atlantic. Flying from New York via Newfoundland, Ireland and England he reached Paris on the following day, to be greeted with tremendous enthusiasm. He was no less popular in England, where he was received at Buckingham Palace by King George.

Photos : Fox and Topical Press

Photo : Central Press

The Menin Gate War Memorial, unveiled by Field-Marshal Lord Plumer on July 24, 1927, at Ypres, in memory of the armies of the British Commonwealth of Nations and of those of their dead who have no known grave. The memorial stands at the entrance to Ypres spanning the " road of death " to the salient, which was held for four years.

Lord Haig of Bemersyde died on January 29th, 1928, and was buried in Dryburgh Abbey. During the greater part of the war he had been Commander-in-Chief of the British forces in France and had won the affection and esteem of his troops and of the nation. He was raised to the peerage in 1919 and granted £100,000 for his services. In addition, the Order of Merit was conferred on him and his ancestral home at Bemersyde bought by public subscription. After the war he became President of the British Legion and organised the sale of poppies on Poppy Day, November 11th, on behalf of disabled Ex-Service Men. On the right Lord Haig is seen in his study at Bemersyde.

Photo : Fox

Many people in London lost their homes and no less than fourteen their lives during the terrible floods of January, 1928. Owing to the meeting of an abnormally high spring tide with a great volume of flood water the Thames suddenly burst its banks at several points, to spread destruction and death over a wide area from Kew right down to the sea.

Photo : Fox

The districts which suffered most were Westminster, Putney and Hammersmith. In many places basements were completely submerged and the pressure of the water caused houses to collapse. Serious damage was done at the Tate Gallery, in the lower part of which hundreds of valuable pictures were stored, among them works by Turner.

On November 21, 1928, the nation learned that King George had a cold with some fever. His illness developed and quickly became critical; and it was not until mid-December that he was out of danger. In February of the following year he was taken to Craigweil House, some two miles from Bognor, where he spent three months convalescing.

Photo : Central Press

Photo : Central Press

In 1929 the Prince of Wales made a tour of the Durham coalfields. He said that the distress and poverty he encountered was "like a nightmare," but that he had been "very deeply touched with the bravery and patience" of the people.

Photo : Fox

Most of the vessels of the German Navy scuttled by their crews at Scapa Flow on June 21, 1919, had by 1930 been brought to the surface. They included the *Hindenburg* (28,000 tons). After being raised the ships were broken up.

Photo : L.N.A. and Wide World

On October 5, 1930, the R 101 crashed near Beauvais in France, while on a flight from Cardington to India. Forty-six persons, including Lord Thomson, Minister for Air, and Air Vice-Marshal Sir Sefton Brancker, lost their lives.

Photo : L.N.A.

" Never before," said King George, in opening the India Round Table Conference on November 12, 1930, " have British and Indian statesmen and rulers of Indian States met, as you now meet, in one place and round one table to discuss the future system of government for India." The Conference decided upon a federal organization.

FASHIONS DURING THE NINETEEN-TWENTIES

The outstanding features of the post-war decade were the variety of hairdressing styles and the fluctuating skirt-length. The examples shown indicate the characteristic low waistline and the rectangular silhouette of the nineteen-twenties. Cloche hats and toques arrived at the same time as severe wide brims and are indicated in the photographs above.

FAVOURITES IN THE ENTERTAINMENT WORLD, 1925-36

(1) Sir Henry Wood, conductor of the B.B.C. " Prom " concerts; (2) Sir H. Walford Davies, Master of the King's Musick; (3) Noel Coward, playwright and actor; (4) Sir Cedric Hardwicke, famous actor; (5) Anna Pavlova, world-famous Russian ballet dancer; (6) Sir Seymour Hicks, popular comedian and playwright; (7) Count John MacCormack, great tenor; (8) Sir Gerald du Maurier, famous actor-manager; (9) Charles Laughton, stage and screen artist; (10) Greta Garbo, screen star; (11) Henry Hall, popular dance band conductor; (12) Gracie Fields, music-hall star.

(1) Lord Burghley, popular athlete; (2) Don Bradman, great Australian cricketer; (3) Bobby Jones, American open golf champion (1930); (4) Amy and (5) Jim Mollison, English flyers; (6) Joyce Wethered, golf champion; (7) Jack Petersen, British heavy-weight boxing champion; (8) Alex. James, Scottish International footballer; (9) Gordon Richards, jockey; (10) Mrs. Helen Wills-Moody and (11) " Bunny " Austin, tennis stars; (12) Miss Mercedes Gleitz, channel swimmer.

(1) A midget motor-car, a ¾-h.p. petrol motor-car with wheels the size of dinner plates, shown with an ordinary taxi-cab; (2) temporary removable barriers erected at Morden Station in 1929 to regulate the flow of passengers on their way to the Epsom Spring Meeting; (3) a G.W.R. record-breaking train; (4) the Graf Zeppelin, the giant German airship, which has maintained a regular service to South America; (5) Dornier Do-X, the largest flying boat ever built; (6) an Armstrong-Whitworth "Argosy" air liner which was in use by Imperial Airways from 1927 to 1932.

(1) J. B. Priestley, novelist and playwright; (2) G. Bernard Shaw, dramatist and sociologist; (3) Frederick Delius, C.H., blind English composer ; (4) Sir John Reith, B.B.C. Director-General ; (5) Sir James Jeans, scientist; (6) Lord Dawson of Penn, physician to his late Majesty; (7) Montagu Norman, Governor of the Bank of England; (8) Margaret Bondfield, Labour leader, first woman Cabinet Minister; (9) Sir Herbert Samuel, Liberal leader; (10) Captain Roald Amundsen, Norwegian Arctic explorer; (11) Lady Astor, first woman M.P.; (12) Mahatma Gandhi, Indian nationalist leader.

The world economic depression which developed in 1929 brought crisis to Britain in the autumn of 1931. In spite of the formation of a National Government composed of members of all three political parties, Great Britain was forced off the gold standard in September. The Government imposed rigid economies in an effort to balance the Budget.

Photos : Central Press and Elliott & Fry

After ten years of preparatory work, the League of Nations Conference on Disarmament was opened at Geneva on February 2, 1932, under the Presidency of Mr. Arthur Henderson (inset). The strain of this work, which he pursued in face of difficulties of every sort, told upon Mr. Henderson's health, and contributed to his untimely death in 1935.

SYDNEY HARBOUR BRIDGE

A triumph of British engineering and Australian workmanship, the gigantic one-span bridge over Sydney Harbour was opened by Mr. Lang, Prime Minister of New South Wales, on March 19, 1932. The bridge has a span of 1,650 feet. In the picture above one of the largest Peninsular and Orient liners has just passed beneath the mammoth structure.

Photo : Wide World

On May 8, 1932, M. Paul Doumer (inset), President of the French Republic, was shot by a mad Russian doctor, Paul Gouguloff, and succumbed to his injuries a few hours later. There was no political motive behind this murder, which robbed France of a scholar and a statesman who had done very valuable work as Governor of Indo-China.

Photo : Fox

An attempt to draw closer the links of Empire trade was made in July, 1932, when an Imperial Economic Conference was opened in the Parliament Buildings at Ottawa, capital of Canada. The imposing Victory Tower shown here stands in the central block of the Parliament Buildings, which were completely reconstructed after the fire of 1916.

Photo : Fox

London's newest bridge, connecting Lambeth with Millbank, was opened by King George on July 19, 1932. Within sight of the Houses of Parliament, it faces some of the largest and most modern of London's office buildings.

Photo : Central Press

The Duke of York was present at the Albert Hall on September 15, 1932, when the representatives of the Wesleyan Methodist, Primitive Methodist and United Methodist Churches met in conference to consummate the union of the three churches. The Rev. Dr. Scott Lidgett, first President of the Methodist Church, is seen signing the deed of Union.

Photo : Keystone

In January, 1933, Adolf Hitler, ex-architect and leader of the Nazi party, was made Chancellor of the German Reich by President Hindenburg, following the failure of Herr von Papen to form a government. Within eighteen months Hitler was dictator of Germany, for Hindenburg died in August, 1934, and the Nazi leader assumed his office.

Photo : Courtesy Houston Everest Expedition

Mount Everest, highest summit on earth (29,141 feet), has so far defied all attempts to scale it, though in 1924 and 1933 mountaineers reached a height of 28,100 feet. On April 3, 1933, the two aeroplanes of the Houston Everest expedition soared over its peak, which they photographed. On April 19 they repeated the exploit.

6...

Photo : Wide World

Late in 1931 Japan invaded Manchuria and within twelve months had driven out the Chinese armies and set up an independent state of Manchukuo. China appealed to the League, a Commission headed by Lord Lytton was sent out, and its report was adopted in February, 1933. Japan thereupon gave notice of withdrawal from the League.

Photo : Fox

The Electricity (Supply) Act of 1926 established the Central Electricity Board to organise and extend the supply of electric power throughout Britain. The Board selected power stations at various points and linked them by a network of transmission lines carried across country by massive steel pylons, such as this one at Dagenham in Essex.

The alarming increase in recent years of road accidents, which in 1934 were responsible for the deaths of over 7,000 people in Britain, and injuries to a quarter of a million, has led to much devising of safety schemes for wheeled traffic and pedestrians. Experts are shown planning how to arrange traffic lights at one of London's busy cross-roads.

Red and green lights at cross-roads were being tried out for the control of wheeled traffic half a dozen years ago, and are now in general use. For pedestrians, nail-studded corridors across streets were first experimented with, followed by the famous " Belisha beacons," now supplemented in a few of the most dangerous places by pedestrian lights.

Photos: Keystone

As early as 1919 King George, speaking to local authorities and voicing a national feeling, said : " It is not merely ' houses ' that are needed. The new houses must be also ' homes.' Can we not aim at securing to the working classes in their homes the comfort, leisure, brightness and peace which we usually associate with the word ' home'?"

During the past fifteen years over a million houses have been built, many of them on pleasant estates and provided with reasonable amenities. Yet in every city and many a town great numbers of people still have to exist in over-crowded and insanitary flats and tenements, with the crowded streets as the only playground for their children.

MODEL HOUSE FOR ROYAL CHILDREN

Photos : Central Press and "The Times"

Princess Elizabeth, who stands second in the line of succession to the throne, in the " grounds " of the Model House presented to her by the people of Wales. On its journey from the Principality the house was somewhat damaged by fire, the thatched roof catching alight. Inset are the Princess and her younger sister, Margaret Rose, born in 1930.

Photos : Central Press and E.N.A.

Albert of the Belgians, a great king both in war and peace, was in his spare time an ardent mountaineer. On February 17, 1934, the world was shocked to hear that he had been killed the previous day while rock-climbing on a pinnacle called the Corneille at Marche les Dames, near Namur. The King's body was found at the spot marked in the foreground.

King Albert, who was in his fifty-ninth year, was greatly beloved by his people, and deeply respected throughout Europe. After the War, in which he led his armies in person, inspiring them with his own courage, he devoted himself with energy to the rebuilding and recreating of his shattered country. The new King, Leopold III, can be clearly seen.

In March, 1934, the Labour Party, for the first time, assumed power in the London County Council, the greatest municipal authority in the world. With Lord Snell (right) as chairman and Mr. Herbert Morrison (left) as leader in the Council Chamber (seen below) their administration has been marked by vigorous and progressive reforms.

Photos : Fox and L.N.A.

One of the new Council's first decisions was to rebuild Waterloo Bridge, and the demolition of the old structure, which had become unsafe owing to the subsidence of one of the piers, was begun in June. The fine new bridge, the design for which is shown here, is not expected to be completed before 1940. Meanwhile a temporary steel bridge is used.

169

Photo : Sport & General

The heat wave of June and July, 1934, following an abnormally dry summer in 1933, faced the country with a serious shortage of water. While holiday-makers revelled in unclouded skies and glorious sunshine and seaside resorts were packed, reservoirs like this at Tring, in Hertfordshire, stood empty, and many villages were entirely without supplies.

Among the charitable efforts to assist those out of work, the National Pilgrimage to the cathedrals in 1934 was inaugurated by King George and Queen Mary, who went to Westminster Abbey on the opening day, July 1.

Photo: Ass. Press

One of the outstanding feats of modern engineering came into service on July 18, 1934, when King George declared open the great motor-road, largest of its kind in the world, which had been tunnelled under the Mersey to link up Liverpool with Birkenhead. Over two miles long, it carries four lines of traffic.

Photos : Central Press and Fox

The year 1934 was unhappy for Austria. I
February, armed resistance by the Socialists t
the Fascist Clerical dictatorship was broken b
heavy shelling of working-class quarters. Man
people were killed. Then in July, Nazis attempte
to seize power. They failed, but not before the
had murdered Dr. Dolfuss, the Chancellor (inset

Photo: Keysto

Photos : Fox

Great distress was caused on Clydeside when, in December, 1931, work was abandoned on the giant Cunard liner "534." Over 3,000 workers were put off, work on the Clyde being reduced by 50 per cent. Many months elapsed before work was resumed, but on September 26, 1934, the vessel was ready for launching. Queen Mary performed the ceremony, and it was officially announced that the liner would sail on her maiden voyage on May 27, 1936.

Photos : Wide World and Sport & Ge

On October 9, 1934, King Alexander of Yugoslavia land
at Marseilles on a political visit to France, and was met
M. Barthou, French Foreign Minister. A few mome
later a man leapt from the crowd on to the runn
board of their car and shot dead both King and Minis

All records for speed were broken in the great Air Race from Mildenhall, Suffolk, to Melbourne in October, 1934, which was won for Great Britain by Messrs. C. W. A. Scott and T. Campbell Black, seen here passing the winning line. They covered 11,323 miles in just under 71 hours.

Photo : Wide World

Photos : Fox and Bassano

Late in August, 1934, came the news that Prince George, while on holiday in Yugoslavia had become engaged to Princess Marina, daughter of Prince and Princess Nicholas of Greece. Amid scenes of enthusiasm their marriage took place in Westminster Abbey on November 29. A few days previously Prince George had been made Duke of Kent.

Sir Malcolm Campbell began his career as a racing motorist in 1910. In 1928 he achieved 200 m.p.h.; since then he has broken record after record in his famous and oft rebuilt *Bluebird*. Early in 1935 he did 280 m.p.h.; in September of the same year, at Bonneville Flats, Utah, U.S.A., he achieved 301.337 m.p.h.

Photo: Keystone

In October, 1934, the *Deutschland* (seen here), first of Germany's " pocket " battleships, visited the Firth of Forth, the first German warship to do so since the War. The third and last of these formidable vessels, which are only of 10,000 tons, but carry six 11-inch guns and have a speed of 26 knots, was commissioned in January, 1936.

Photo : Topical

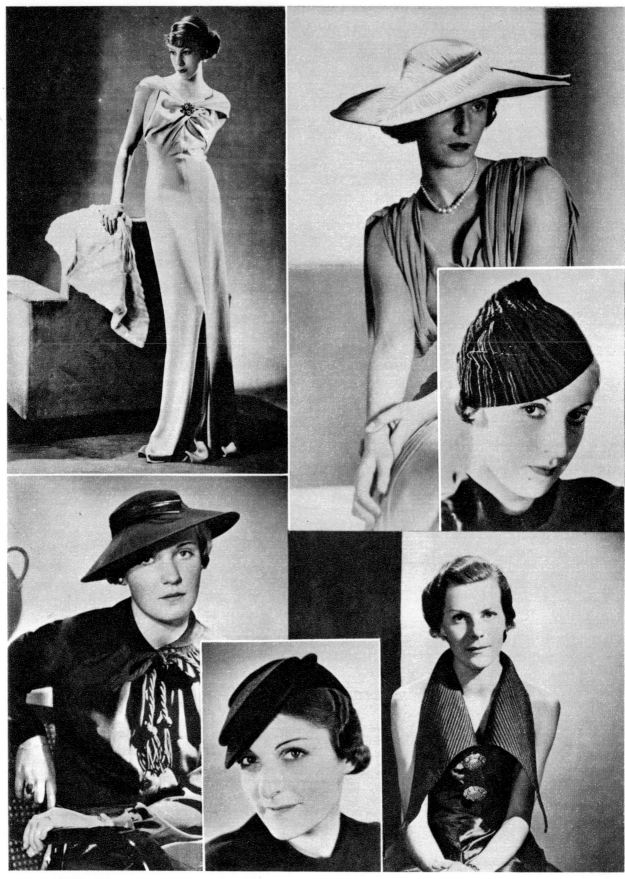

Skirts lengthened and long graceful lines became the mode, culminating in the " Greek " robes of spring, 1936. Hats, which had shrunk to pill-box size (lower middle) about 1934, grew larger. The shape shown at the left became fashionable. At the same time an element of fantasy appeared in the tailoring of evening clothes (see lower right picture). Simplicity and elegance of line has taken the place of over-ornamentation and grotesque shapes—but for how long?

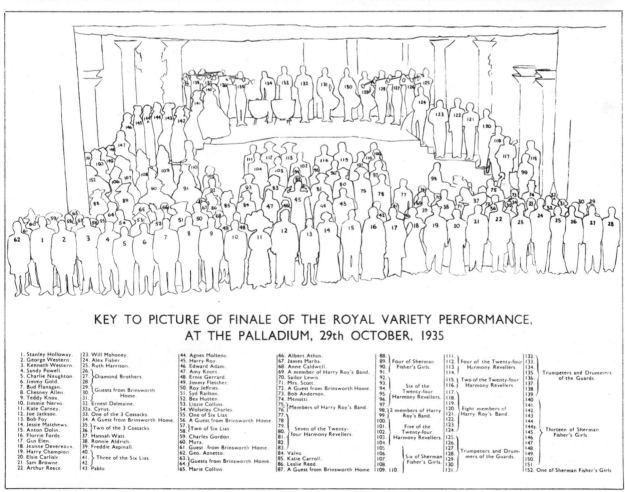

KEY TO PICTURE OF FINALE OF THE ROYAL VARIETY PERFORMANCE, AT THE PALLADIUM, 29th OCTOBER, 1935

1. Stanley Holloway.
2. George Western.
3. Kenneth Western.
4. Sandy Powell.
5. Charlie Naughton.
6. Jimmy Gold.
7. Bud Flanagan.
8. Chesney Allen.
9. Teddy Knox.
10. Jimmie Nervo.
11. Kate Carney.
12. Joe Jackson.
13. Bob Foy.
14. Jessie Matthews.
15. Anton Dolin.
16. Florrie Forde.
17. Gus Elen.
18. Jeanne Devereaux.
19. Harry Champion.
20. Elsie Carlisle.
21. Sam Browne.
22. Arthur Reece.

23. Will Mahoney.
24. Alex Fisher.
25. Ruth Harrison.
26. }
27. } Diamond Brothers
28. }
29. }
30. } Guests from Brinsworth Home.
31. }
32. Ernest Dalmaine.
32a. Cyrus.
33. One of the 3 Cossacks.
34. A Guest from Brinsworth Home.
35. }
36. } Two of the 3 Cossacks.
37. Hannah Watt.
38. Ronnie Aldrich.
39. Freddie Aspinall.
40. }
41. } Three of the Six Lias.
42. }
43. Pablo

44. Agnes Moltenc.
45. Harry Roy.
46. Edward Adam.
47. Amy Knott.
48. Ernie Gerrard.
49. Jimmy Fletcher.
50. Roy Jeffries.
51. Syd Railton.
52. Bea Hutten.
53. Lizzie Collins.
54. Wolseley Charles.
55. One of Six Lias.
56. A Guest from Brinsworth Home.
57. }
58. } Two of Six Lias.
59. Charles Gordon.
60. Mura.
61. Guest from Brinsworth Home.
62. Geo. Aznetto.
63. }
64. } Guests from Brinsworth Home.
65. Marie Collins.

66. Albert Athos.
67. James Marba.
68. Anne Caldwell.
69. A member of Harry Roy's Band.
70. Sailor Lewis.
71. Mrs. Scott.
72. A Guest from Brinsworth Home.
73. Bob Anderson.
74. Menotti.
75. }
76. } Members of Harry Roy's Band.
77. }
78. }
79. } Seven of the Twenty-
80. } four Harmony Revellers.
81. }
82. }
83. }
84. Valvo.
85. Katie Carroll.
86. Leslie Reed.
87. A Guest from Brinsworth Home

88. }
89. } Four of Sherman
90. } Fisher's Girls.
91. }
92. }
93. } Six of the
94. } Twenty-four
95. } Harmony Revellers.
96. }
97. }
98. } 2 members of Harry
99. } Roy's Band.
100. }
101. } Five of the
102. } Twenty-four
103. } Harmony Revellers.
104. }
105. }
106. }
107. } Six of Sherman
108. } Fisher's Girls.
109. 110.

111. }
112. } Four of the Twenty-four
113. } Harmony Revellers.
114. }
115. } Two of the Twenty-four
116. } Harmony Revellers.
117. }
118. }
119. }
120. } Eight members of
121. } Harry Roy's Band.
122. }
123. }
124. }
125. }
126. }
127. }
128. } Trumpeters and Drum-
129. } mers of the Guards.
130. }
131. }

132. }
133. }
134. }
135. } Trumpeters and Drummers
136. } of the Guards.
137. }
138. }
139. }
140. }
141. }
142. }
143. }
144. }
144a. }
145. } Thirteen of Sherman
146. } Fisher's Girls.
147. }
148. }
149. }
150. }
151. }
152. One of Sherman Fisher's Girls

The distinctive feature of the most modern forms of transport is streamlining, which minimises wind resistance and results in increased speed and economy of fuel. The new monsters of road and rail have a strange beauty of their own, as will be seen from some of the pictures above. (1) A view of the front of an experimental type of streamlined bus on the London streets; (2) a streamlined luxury motor-coach; and (3) the Silver Link, the latest type of streamlined locomotive on the L.N.E.R. Pictures 4, 5, and 6 illustrate the latest types of aeroplanes; (4) the *Hengist*, an Imperial Airways air liner; (5) the *Scipio*, a flying-boat on the India air route; and (6) an autogyro.

(1) Stanley Baldwin, Prime Minister, 1923, 1924–29, and since 1935; (2) Viscount Snowden of Ickornshaw, former Socialist Cabinet Minister; (3) Mr. Attlee, leader of Labour Party in House of Commons; (4) Dame Ethel Smythe, famous English composer and conductor; (5) Sir Edwin Lutyens, celebrated architect; (6) Dame Laura Knight, R.A., English painter; (7) Rudyard Kipling, poet of Empire; (8) John Masefield, Poet Laureate; (9) John L. Baird, inventor of a method of television; (10) George Lansbury, Socialist leader and former Cabinet Minister; (11) M. Litvinov, Soviet Secretary for Foreign Affairs; (12) Franklin D. Roosevelt, President of the U.S.A.

Photo: Ass. Press

For months during 1934 King George was kept busy over the arrangements for the celebration of his Silver Jubilee. In February he and Queen Mary went on holiday to Eastbourne in preparation for their strenuous round of Jubilee engagements. They stayed at Compton Place, which was put at their disposal by the Duke and Duchess of Devonshire.

Photo : Sport & General

London began to wear a festive air some time before the Jubilee celebrations commenced. Visitors crowded into the city, stands were erected along the routes to be taken by the Royal processions, and streets were made gay with flags and streamers. Slum areas were decorated as vividly if not as expensively as Regent Street, seen in this picture.

Photo : Fox

On the morning of May 6, 1935, the twenty-fifth anniversary of the accession of King George, the King and Queen rode between vast crowds of cheering people to a Thanksgiving Service at St. Paul's Cathedral. Many of the spectators came from distant parts of the Empire. Their Majesties passing down Fleet Street on their way to the Cathedral.

Photo : P.N.A.

The service in the Cathedral was simple in character, consisting of well-known hymns and psalms with a brief but impressive address by the Archbishop of Canterbury. As the congregation had to be restricted to official representatives and distinguished guests, a second service for the general public was held during the afternoon.

Unprecedented scenes were witnessed in London on Jubilee night. All roads led to Buckingham Palace, in front of which a crowd estimated at 250,000 gathered. The King came out on the balcony shortly after nine o'clock, but long after this thousands of people continued to swell the throng. In response to their appeals he appeared again at ten t

Photo: British Inter. P.P.A.

ven, to be greeted by the vast concourse of people with tremendous and sustained cheering. Then the crowd slowly
persed, some to their homes, others to sing and dance in Trafalgar Square, Piccadilly, and other open spaces and
in thoroughfares. Well-known dance bands led the revelry, which was prolonged till the early hours of the morning.

HIS MAJESTY'S MESSAGE TO HIS PEOPLES

BROADCAST FROM BUCKINGHAM PALACE
AT 8 P.M., 6TH MAY, 1935

AT the close of this memorable day I must speak to my people everywhere. Yet how can I express what is in my heart? As I passed this morning through cheering multitudes to and from St. Paul's Cathedral, as I thought there of all that these twenty-five years have brought to me and to my country and my Empire, how could I fail to be most deeply moved? Words cannot express my thoughts and feelings. I can only say to you, my very dear people, that the Queen and I thank you from the depth of our hearts for all the loyalty and—may I say?—the love with which this day and always you have surrounded us. I dedicate myself anew to your service for the years that may still be given to me.

I look back on the past with thankfulness to God. My people and I have come through great trials and difficulties together. They are not over. In the midst of this day's rejoicing I grieve to think of the numbers of my people who are still without work. We owe to them, and not least to those who are suffering from any form of disablement, all the sympathy and help we can give. I hope that

during this Jubilee Year all who can will do their utmost to find them work and bring them hope.

Other anxieties may be in store. But I am persuaded that with God's help they may all be overcome, if we meet them with confidence, courage and unity. So I look forward to the future with faith and hope.

It is to the young that the future belongs. I trust that through the Fund inaugurated by my dear son, the Prince of Wales, to commemorate this year, many of them throughout this country may be helped in body, mind, and character to become useful citizens.

To the children I would like to send a special message. Let me say this to each of them whom my words may reach : The King is speaking to *you*. I ask you to remember that in days to come you will be the citizens of a great Empire. As you grow up always keep this thought before you ; and when the time comes be ready and proud to give to your country the service of your work, your mind and your heart.

I have been greatly touched by all the greetings which have come to me to-day from my Dominions and Colonies, from India and from this home country. My heart goes out to all who may be listening to me now wherever you may be—here at home in town or village, or in some far off corner of the Empire, or it may be on the high seas.

Let me end my words to you with those which Queen Victoria used after her Diamond Jubilee, thirty-eight years ago. No words could more truly or simply express my own deep feeling now : "From my heart I thank my beloved people. May God bless them."

Photo : "The Times"

On May 9, the King and Queen drove to the historic Westminster Hall, where they received Jubilee addresses of congratulation from both Houses of Parliament, presented respectively by the Lord Chancellor, Viscount Sankey, and the Speaker of the House of Commons, Captain Fitzroy. His Majesty is seen replying to the addresses.

Photo : Fox

On May 11, 1935, the King's sons went respectively to Wales, Scotland and Northern Ireland for special Jubilee celebrations. At Cardiff the Prince of Wales had a great reception, especially from the 45,000 school children gathered in Cardiff Arms Park. The day was described as "Wales's greatest since the investiture of the Prince of Wales."

Photo : Fox

Children also figured prominently in the celebrations at Edinburgh, 20,000 of them taking part in a " March of Youth " demonstration on the Rugby Union ground at Murrayfield. The Duke of York, who was accompanied by the Duchess, delivered a special speech thanking them for their message of loyalty and homage to the King.

Photo : Fox

The Duke of Gloucester, who is also Earl of Ulster, represented King George at Belfast, where he attended a youth pageant presented by more than 8,000 members of the Boys' Brigade, Boy Scouts and Girl Guides. During his stay in Northern Ireland he visited Londonderry, where he received the Freedom of the " Maiden City."

7.

Photo : " The Times "

Very popular features of the Jubilee celebrations were the four processional drives which their Majesties made through North, South, East and West London. The drives were made on Saturday afternoons so that the maximum number of people could see them, and by their Majesties' special request places were always reserved for school children.

Photo : L.N.A.

Most delightful, though quite unofficial, were the many Jubilee tea parties held in London's poorer streets. The children collected money, their parents did the cooking, and obliging friends and neighbours lent tea-urns, trestle-tables, chairs, forms, and pianos. Each street strove to be the best decorated, and some of the displays of bunting were most lavish.

Photo : Fox

Extensive floodlighting was a feature of the Jubilee celebrations. Most of London's prominent buildings were floodlit, including the Royal Palaces, Westminster Abbey, St. Paul's Cathedral, London County Hall, the National Gallery, Mansion House and Royal Exchange. The illumination of the Admiralty Arch (seen here) was particularly admired.

Photo : Fox

The bridges at Richmond, Hampton Court and Hammersmith were illuminated, while on the Thames the training ship *President* was a mass of light. In June St. James's Park was floodlit with exquisite effect. All over the country famous buildings, including castles, cathedrals, churches, city halls, and monuments, were illuminated.

In every part of the Empire the Silver Jubilee was celebrated with impressive state and cordial demonstrations of loyalty and affection. In Canada a crowd of more than 50,000 people gathered on Parliament Hill at Ottawa for a grand Thanksgiving Service, at which the Governor-General, Lord Bessborough, read a message from the King.

Photos : Wide World and " The Times "

Throughout India prayers were offered for Their Majesties in Hindu temples and Mohammedan mosques. At Delhi, where the Viceroy and Lady Willingdon were present for the celebrations, five miles of illuminations blazed into the night, while at Bombay and Calcutta impressive processions were followed by feasting and scenes of rejoicing.

Photo : Central Press

Greatest of all permanent memorials of the Silver Jubilee is the King George's Jubilee Trust Fund inaugurated by the Prince of Wales to assist youth organisations throughout the country. " A nation's youth is a nation's future," said the Prince in a radio appeal for subscriptions, which produced the largest sum ever received from a broadcast.

Photo : Vandyke

On August 29, 1935 the beautiful Queen Astrid, consort of the young King of the Belgians, was killed in a motoring accident in Switzerland. Queen Astrid, who was thirty years old and a niece of the King of Sweden, is seen here with her children (left to right) Princess Josephine Charlotte, Prince Albert and the Crown Prince Baudouin.

Photo : L.N.A.

Deep sympathy was felt for King Leopold, who less than two years previously had lost his father as the result of a mountaineering accident. King Leopold, who was driving the car when it crashed into a stone parapet near Kusnacht, a resort on the beautiful Lake Zurich, was himself injured and appeared at the funeral with his arm in a sling.

Photo : News Service, Inc.

A photograph taken in 1935 of the world-famous quintuplets, born on May 28, 1934 at Callander, Ontario, to Mrs. Elzire Dionne. Thanks to extraordinary medical skill and devoted nursing, all were successfully reared, a specially constructed hospital being built to house them. Left to right: Annette, Emilie, Cecile, Yvonne and Marie.

Photo : Topical

All records for ascents into the stratosphere were broken on November 11, 1935, when two United States Army officers reached a height of 74,187 feet. They took off at Rapid City, South Dakota in a metal ball nine feet in diameter attached to a balloon as high as a twenty-storey building, and landed safely at White Lake, 230 miles east.

After many months of preparation and in defiance of the League of Nations, Italy invaded Abyssinia in October, 1935. Abyssinia appealed to the League, which declared Italy to be the aggressor, and fixed a date upon which, should Italy not give way, economic sanctions would be imposed by States members. In November sanctions were begun.

Photos : Sport & General and Topical

Britain gave a strong lead at Geneva for the principle of collective security until December, when the terms of a proposed pact arranged by France and Britain were strongly criticized. This pact, which offered Italy more than generous concessions, led to the resignation of Sir Samuel Hoare (left inset) as Foreign Secretary, who is seen above addressing a conference at Geneva. He was succeeded by Mr. Anthony Eden, who is shown on the right.

Photo : Cameragrams P.A.

Neither threats nor concessions moved the Dictator of Italy from his warlike path. While the League debated, Mussolini dispatched more troops to East Africa, and in a series of fiery speeches roused Italy to a pitch of fervour. Britain he accused of partisanship, and the imposition of sanctions he said he would regard as an " unfriendly act."

The Italian troops won a series of initial successes in northern Abyssinia, capturing Adowa, the scene of their defeat in 1896, the holy city of Aksum, and Makale. Their troops in the south also penetrated to a considerable depth. But the necessity of building roads and of protecting their communications made further progress slow. In these pictures are shown typical Abyssinian soldiers.

Photo : Keystone

The Abyssinians, inadequately armed and unskilled in modern warfare, lived up to their reputation as guerilla fighters, and inflicted considerable losses upon the Italian troops, ambushing outposts and supply columns, and retiring into the hills whenever the main force of the enemy advanced. Experience taught them how to meet hostile air-raids.

Photo : Keystone

The wedding of the Duke of Gloucester, third son of the King, to Lady Alice Montagu-Douglas-Scott took place on November 6, 1935. Owing to the recent death of the bride's father, the Duke of Buccleuch, the preparations for an Abbey wedding were cancelled, and the ceremony took place quietly in the Chapel of Buckingham Palace.

The honeymoon was spent at Boughton House, the Northamptonshire seat of the Dukes of Buccleuch, and at Quenby Hall, Leicestershire, where for a week the royal couple were the guests of Sir Harold Nutting, Master of the Quorn Hunt. Afterwards they went to Ulster, where they were entertained as the guests of Sir Basil and Lady Brooke.

In November, 1935, the monarchy was restored in Greece, which had been a republic since 1924. King George II, who had been living in exile in England, was seen off in London by the Prince of Wales, and received in Athens by General Kondylis, who had been mainly instrumental in securing his return, but who died soon after.

King George was the first monarch to speak to his subjects through the medium of wireless. On Christmas Day, 1932, he broadcast from Sandringham a message " to all my peoples throughout the Empire." On each succeeding Christmas of his life he did the same. His last message, spoken shortly before his death, is given on the opposite page.

Photo : " The Times "

KING GEORGE'S
LAST CHRISTMAS MESSAGE
25TH DECEMBER, 1935

 WISH you all, my dear friends, a happy Christmas. I have been deeply touched by the greetings which in the last few minutes have reached me from all parts of the Empire. Let me in response send to each of you a greeting from myself. My words will be very simple but spoken from the heart on this family festival of Christmas.

The year that is passing—the twenty-fifth since my Accession—has been to me most memorable. It called forth a spontaneous offering of loyalty—and may I say of love—which the Queen and I can never forget. How could I fail to note in all the rejoicing not merely respect for the Throne but a warm and generous remembrance of the man himself who, may God help him, has been placed upon it.

It is this personal link between me and my people which I value more than I can say. It binds us together in all our common joys and sorrows, as when this year you showed your happiness in the marriage of my son, and your sympathy in the death of my beloved sister. I feel this link now as I speak to you. For I am thinking not so much of the Empire itself as of the individual men, women and children who live within it, whether they are dwelling here at home or in some distant outpost of the Empire.

In Europe and many parts of the world anxieties surround us. It is good to think that our own family of peoples is at peace in itself and united in one desire to be at peace with other nations—the friend of all, the enemy of none. May the spirit of good will and mutual helpfulness grow and spread. Then it will bring not only the blessing of peace but a solution of the economic troubles which still beset us.

To those who are suffering or in distress, whether in this country or in any part of the Empire, I offer my deepest sympathy. But I would also give a Christmas message of hope and cheer. United by the bonds of willing service, let us prove ourselves both strong to endure and resolute to overcome.

Once again as I close I send to you all, and not the least to the children who may be listening to me, my truest Christmas wishes, and those of my dear wife, my children, and grandchildren who are with me to-day. I add a heartfelt prayer that, wherever you are, God may bless and keep you always.

Sandringham House, Norfolk, the country seat of King George. Following his usual custom, King George went here for Christmas, and from here made his last broadcast. On Friday, January 17, 1936, it was announced that His Majesty had a cold, with some fever. At first the illness was not regarded as serious.

Photo : Graphic Photo Union

A bulletin issued on Friday night spoke of " cardiac weakness," and expressed anxiety. By Saturday morning it became apparent that the King's illness was of a grave character, and the Princesses Elizabeth and Margaret Rose, who had been spending the Christmas holidays at Sandringham with their grandfather, returned to London.

On Sunday in every church throughout the Empire prayers were offered up for the King's recovery, while during the evening special prayers and intercession for His Majesty were broadcast. The bulletins that day were more hopeful, for they stated that the King had maintained his strength and that there was no change in his condition.

Many people visited the beautiful parish church at Sandringham, where the rector announced at morning service that he was authorised to say that the King was slightly stronger than on Saturday. Yet the fact that none of the Royal Family was present showed how seriously the King's illness was regarded.

Photo : Fox

The first bulletin on Monday, January 20, created a hopeful atmosphere, for it said that " The King has had a more rest
night. There is no substantial change to record in His Majesty's condition." But change came during the day, and swift
At 5.30 p.m. came the ominous news that " The condition of His Majesty the King shows diminishing strength." Everyo

Photo : Fox

emed to sense that this was the beginning of the end, and during the evening large crowds of silent and anxious people
thered outside Buckingham Palace, or listened tensely for the frequent broadcast reports. No further news came until
5 p.m., when the world learned with intense grief that " The King's life is moving peacefully towards its close."

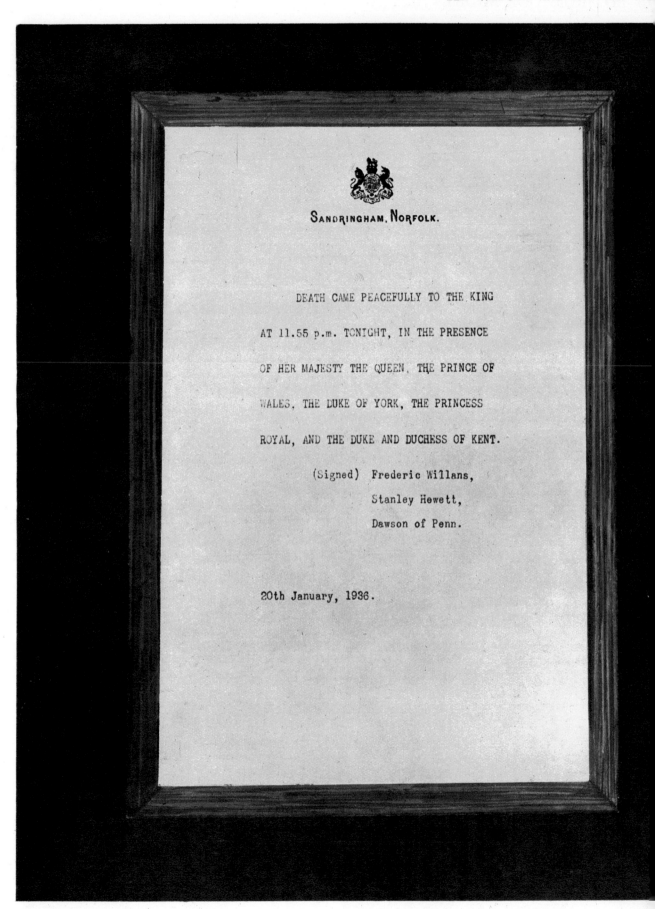

SANDRINGHAM, NORFOLK.

DEATH CAME PEACEFULLY TO THE KING

AT 11.55 p.m. TONIGHT, IN THE PRESENCE

OF HER MAJESTY THE QUEEN, THE PRINCE OF

WALES, THE DUKE OF YORK, THE PRINCESS

ROYAL, AND THE DUKE AND DUCHESS OF KENT.

(Signed) Frederic Willans,

Stanley Hewett,

Dawson of Penn.

20th January, 1936.

The end came at five minutes to twelve, and was announced shortly after midnight. The waiting crowds outside the Pal
saw a solitary figure walk across the courtyard, remove one notice from the rails and replace it by another. A man read
and removed his hat. The best loved monarch in the world was dead. Women sobbed quietly, or knelt in prayer on

Photos : L.N.A.

vement; men stood silent with bared heads and downcast eyes. Then slowly, almost without a word, the throng began to elt away into the darkness. Meanwhile, a countless host of listeners at home and abroad, had heard the quiet voice Sir John Reith telling all parts of the Empire that " He whom we loved as King has passed from our midst."

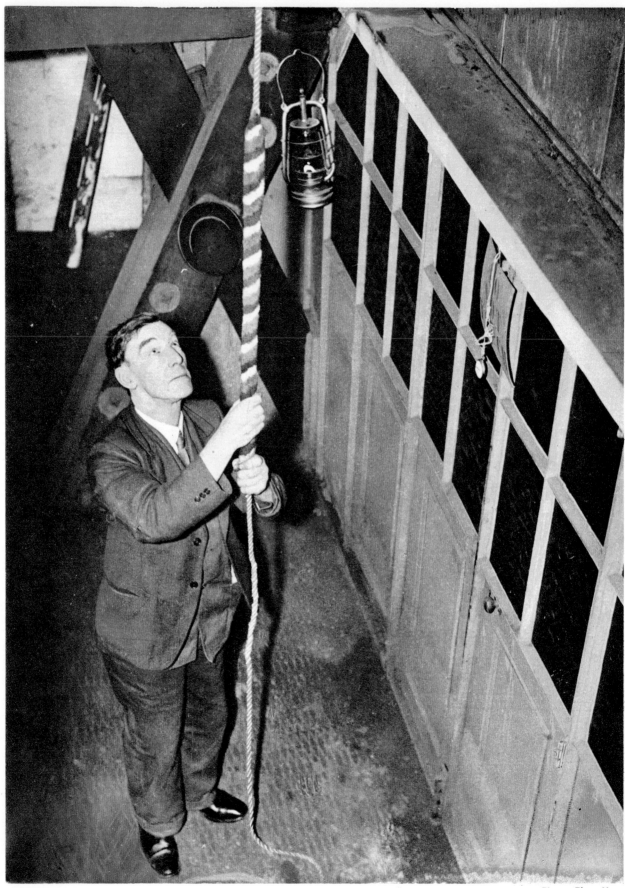

Photo : Planet News

London on Wednesday was transformed into a city of mourning. At 8 o'clock in the morning, " Great Tom," the big bell of St. Paul's Cathedral, boomed out its sombre note, to be continued at one-minute intervals for two hours. At midday a great congregation of City workers gathered in the Cathedral for a brief memorial service.

Photo : *Graphic Photo Union*

In **Hyde Park** and at the **Tower** of London the roar of artillery paid impressive salute to departed majesty. Seventy times—once for each year of the late King's life—at one-minute intervals, the guns gave tongue. In the Park the gunners wore full dress uniform, while at the Tower the guns were lined to face the waters of the Thames.

Photo : L.N.A.

All over the city flags flew at half-mast; on the Victoria Tower of the Houses of Parliament, at the Admiralty, where it is so flown only when the Sovereign passes, from the west front of Westminster Abbey, above all government offices, and on innumerable other buildings, public and private; even to humble shops in unfashionable thoroughfares.

218

Photo : Camera portrait by Hugh Cecil

On Wednesday the flags fluttered again to the masthead, while with traditional ceremony heralds proclaimed the accession of " our only lawful and rightful Liege Lord Edward the Eighth." In London the Proclamation was made, according to custom, first at St. James's Palace, and later at Charing Cross, Temple Bar and the Royal Exchange.

Photo : " The Times "

From Tuesday night until Thursday morning the King's body reposed in the parish church of St. Mary Magdalene, at Sandringham. The coffin, made of Sandringham oak, was borne from Sandringham House by woodmen and game-keepers on the Royal estate, who, after its arrival at the church, mounted guard, four at a time, over the simple catafalque.

Photo : Ass. Press

The late King's affection for animals was well known, and his white shooting pony, Jock, was among his favourites. Only a few days before his death His Majesty had been out riding on Jock, which had been his constant mount for twelve years.   Jock lived at Windsor, but was always taken to Balmoral or Sandringham when the King went there.

On Thursday morning, January 23, after a brief service in Sandringham Church, the last sad journey to London begun. Beneath a sky of cloudless blue the simple cortège wended its way through the woods to Wolferton stati two-and-a-half miles distant. The new King, bareheaded, walked just behind the coffin, followed by his broth

Photo : L.N.A.

Lord Harewood. After them came two carriages bearing Queen Mary and the Royal ladies. The only music heard ore the procession reached the railway station was the wailing note of the lament played by the King's Piper during passage through Sandringham Park. Villagers walked beside the mourners as they passed along the country roads.

Photo : " The Times "

On the coffin, which was borne on a gun-carriage escorted by Grenadier Guardsmen, were placed two wreaths only, from Queen Mary and her family. Behind the Royal mourners walked tenants and servants of the estate. At Wolferton station Norfolk territorials formed a guard of honour, while men of the British Legion lined the road.

Photo : " The Times "

At King's Cross all sound of traffic had been stilled before the Royal train glided silently into the station. King Edward assisted his mother to alight from the train, the Princess Royal adjusted the wreaths on the coffin, and the Royal mourners stood by the open doors of the funeral coach as the King's body was borne out into the streets of London.

Photo : Fox

Dense crowds of silent people watched the brief procession, shorn of almost every semblance of state in its simple majesty, which accompanied the King's body to Westminster. The Imperial Crown, the wreaths, and the Royal Standard on the coffin were almost the only touches of colour; mounted police and Guardsmen the sole escort.

Almost all the people who lined the route wore some sign of mourning, and hardly a sound broke the stillness as cortège passed. Outside King's Cross the dense crowd was composed mainly of poorer people, many of whom waited patiently for hours. In Kingsway, Aldwych, and the Strand business was abandoned; offices and sl

Photo : L.N.A.

e closed and neon lights were put out. In Trafalgar Square the pale rays of the setting sun lit up a vast concourse
areheaded and reverent mourners as the gun-carriage with its burden passed almost within the shadow of Nelson's
mn. The very simplicity of the little procession seemed to add solemnity to the passing of a great King.

Photo : L.N.A.

In Whitehall the silence was most impressive. As the procession reached the Cenotaph the Guards, passing on the left of it, turned heads to the right in salute to the fallen. King Edward, his brothers and the members of the Royal household paid the same tribute, and the cortège passed on towards Parliament Square and the historic Westminster Hall.

228

Photo : Sport and General

All along the route, from King's Cross to Westminster, there breathed as it were a sigh of deepest sympathy for the new King whose drawn set face marked the tense strain he felt. With him walked the Dukes of York and Gloucester.

Photo : L.N.A.

Outside Westminster Hall the coffin was received by the Archbishop of Canterbury, the Lord Great Chamberlain, the Earl Marshal and the First Commissioner of Works. As it was carried into the Hall the Union Jack on the Victoria Tower of the House of Lords fluttered down, and the Royal Standard was hoisted at half mast in its place.

Photo : Fox

The bearers laid the coffin on the catafalque; the Archbishop offered prayer; a choir sang " Praise my soul, the King of Heaven "; the words of the Benediction were heard : " The Lord lift up the light of His countenance upon thee, and give thee peace, now and for evermore," and the old Hall was left to departed Majesty and its silent guard.

Early on Friday morning the doors of Westminster Hall were opened to the public, and for four days an endless stream of mourners filed past the dead King as he lay in state. Young and old, rich and poor, of every rank and calling, King George's subjects thronged to pay a final tribute to him who throughout his eventful reign was " one of us."

Photo : L.N.A.

On Sunday, January 26, a scene passing description unfolded itself, for as the day wore on the vast queue of pilgrims to Westminster grew ever longer. By the afternoon it stretched the length of Millbank, across Vauxhall Bridge, and back to Westminster Bridge, forming a solid block of people three miles long and in places sixteen to twenty deep.

Photo : Fox

So enormous was the waiting multitude that it was decided to keep the doors of Westminster Hall open until the early hours of Monday morning, and the last mourners actually passed through shortly before 4 a.m. Altogether during the four days of the lying-in-state over three-quarters of a million people filed past the catafalque.

Photo : L.N.A.

Special arrangements were made by the police, who throughout handled the enormous queues with unfailing courtesy and skill, in order that all disabled persons arriving in wheeled chairs should be allowed to enter the Hall by the entrance in Palace Yard, thus avoiding steps or any danger of being crushed or jostled. Many gratefully accepted.

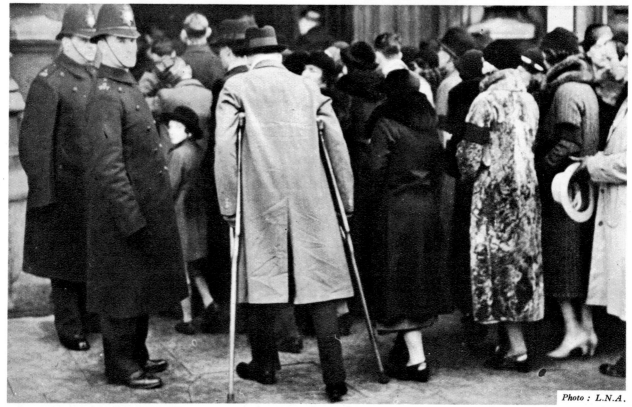

Photo : L.N.A.

Other crippled folk on crutches were to be seen in the queue, enduring the long wait and the slow dragging progress as stoically as the rest. There were some pathetic scenes, especially on Sunday night, when people waited eight hours to enter the Hall, as exhausted pilgrims fell fainting to the ground within a few hundred yards of their goal.

The Route of the
FUNERAL
PROCESSION
of His Late Majesty
KING GEORGE V
from Westminster Hall to Paddington
January 28th 1936

By midnight on Monday thousands of people had taken up positions from which to view the funeral of King George, and by two o'clock on Tuesday morning they could be counted in tens of thousands. Many of them went straight from passing through Westminster Hall to Parliament Square, Whitehall, the Mall (seen here), Piccadilly and other places along the route, where they camped out for the remaining hours, quite undeterred by the drizzling rain.

Photos : Fox

At a quarter to ten on Tuesday the King's coffin, draped in the Royal Standard, and bearing the Regalia, was brought out from Westminster Hall and placed on the gun-carriage, and the journey was begun.

Photos : Sport & General and Fox

Photo : Fox

At a given signal the long procession, which had been forming for an hour or more, began to move forward. Behind the gun-carriage the Royal Standard was borne by a warrant officer of the Household Cavalry; then came King Edward VIII, in naval uniform with greatcoat, followed by his brothers, the Dukes of York, Gloucester and Kent.

Photo : L.N.A.

After the mourners on foot came the great glass coach bearing Queen Mary, the scarlet trappings of its coachman and footmen in vivid contrast with the sombre hues of both procession and crowd. Immediately behind the coach walked High Commissioners, representatives of foreign states and foreign delegations, naval, military and civil.

Photo : L.N.A

Five kings and many princes from abroad followed King George to his last resting place. In the picture are seen (left to right) King Haakon of Norway, the Crown Prince of Norway, the Earl of Athlone (behind whom is King Carol of Rumania), King Christian of Denmark, King Leopold of the Belgians, M. Lebrun, President of the French Republic, the Prince of Piedmont, King Boris of Bulgaria, the Prince Regent of Yugoslavia, and the Crown Prince of Sweden.

Photo : Fox

The historic gun-carriage, on which had been borne the bodies of Queen Victoria and King Edward VII, was drawn the four miles that separate Westminster from Paddington by a gun's crew of five officers and 142 men from Chatham. They marched with faultless precision in ranks of eight, 98 manning the drag ropes ahead, 40 those astern.

The massed bands of the Brigade of Guards, the bands of the Royal Air Force, the Royal Marines, the Royal Engineers, the Royal Artillery, together with a combined pipe band from Scottish and Irish regiments, and the bands of the 3rd Carabiniers and the Household Cavalry played solemn music from Westminster to Paddington.

Photo : Fox

Overwhelming crowds had gathered at every point along the route taken by the funeral procession, and in several place: cordon of police and troops was broken. By nine o'clock in the morning the large open space at the Marble Arch completely filled, and people were still trying to pour in in their thousands. Shortly before the procession was due to j

ne of troops facing the Bayswater Road broke under the pressure, and for some moments the route was entirely blocked,
confusion reigned, heightened by the cries of those who had the misfortune to be in the worst of the crush. It is esti-
d on competent authority that 100,000 people were gathered at this place, one of the largest crowds ever seen.

At Paddington station the stands had been draped in royal purple. Owing to the crowds the procession was half an hour late, and the head of it did not reach the station till just before noon. As the bearers carried the coffin to the train, a band in the distance played "O Rest in the Lord."

Photo : Photopress

Five special trains bearing distinguished visitors, statesmen and ambassadors preceded the Royal train bearing the coffin and the Royal party to Windsor. Along the line groups of people had gathered at every point of vantage to pay a last and fleeting tribute of homage to their late King. The train reached Windsor shortly after one o'clock.

Photo : Fox

In the grounds at Windsor thousands of floral tributes sent from all over the country were laid out on the green sward. They varied from costly and elaborate garlands to humble bunches of violets and snowdrops. Every token was accorded a place. After the funeral hundreds of thousands of people visited Windsor to see the wonderful display.

Minute guns heralded the arrival of the Royal train at Windsor. The coffin was borne to the gun-carriage, and while crew of men from the *Excellent* stood bareheaded, the bosun's whistle piped first the call "Admiral Alongside," and w the coffin was placed on the gun-carriage, "Admiral Aboard." Then, to the strains of the Funeral March, the proces wound its way up the steep street of old Windsor and into the castle grounds. As in London, King Edward VIII wal

Photo : P.N.A.

ne immediately behind the coffin, followed by his brothers and the foreign sovereigns and princes. A single carriage
nveyed Queen Mary, Queen Maud of Norway, the Princess Royal, the Duchess of York, and Princess Elizabeth. Then
ne thirty-five foreign representatives, including Mr. Norman Davis of the United States and M. Maxim Litvinoff,
ief of the Russian Mission. A two-minute silence was observed throughout the Empire between 1.30 and 1.32 p.m.

At length the head of the procession came in sight of the historic Chapel of St. George's, Windsor, burial place of Br
Kings, and among the most exquisite examples of Perpendicular architecture in the country. It was begun by Edward
the first King to be buried there, and was completed by Henry VIII. During the reign of King George V it was found

Photo : " The Times"

roof with its magnificent fan-vaulting was in a serious condition of decay, and extensive restoration had to be carried at considerable cost. St. George's is the Chapel of the Knights of the Garter, whose stalls are in the Chancel. The of the King, who is Sovereign of the Order, was empty throughout the ceremony, while that of Queen Mary was draped.

Photo : Fox

At the main entrance of the Chapel waited the Archbishop of Canterbury, the Dean of Windsor, the Archbishop of York and the Canons of the Chapel. As the coffin reached the foot of the steps the bos'n's whistle " piped over the side " the Lord High Admiral, and to the wailing notes of a Highland lament the coffin entered the Chapel.

Photo : Fox

Led by the choir and the clergy, the cortège moved slowly up the nave of St. George's and into the chancel, the choir chanting the glorious words of everlasting hope, " I am the Resurrection and the Life," and " I know that my Redeemer liveth." The coffin was gently placed upon a bier at the foot of the altar steps and the regalia removed.

Photo : Fox

King Edward and Queen Mary stood behind the coffin. The choir sang "The Lord is my Shepherd," the Bishop of Winchester read the lesson, and the choir sang softly King George's favourite hymn, "Abide with Me." Then the Archbishop of Canterbury spoke the words preceding committal, and the coffin slowly disappeared from view.

Photo : Fox

King Edward moved forward and scattered a handful of dust upon the coffin in the vault. " Earth to earth, ashes to ashes, dust to dust " . . . and so King George was committed to his last resting place, " in the sure and certain hope of the resurrection to eternal life." His honoured memory remains in our hearts as " a man greatly beloved."

TO THE CHILDREN

A MESSAGE SENT TO THE CHILDREN BY HIS LATE MAJESTY
KING GEORGE V ON THE OCCASION OF THE
25TH ANNIVERSARY OF HIS
ACCESSION TO THE THRONE

YOU are the heirs of a great past; but the future is yours, and is your high responsibility. Each of you must try to be a good citizen in a good city. To this end, you must make the best of all your powers. Strive to grow in strength, in knowledge, and in grace. If you persist bravely in this endeavour you will work worthily for your family, your city, your country, and for mankind. So to live, in whatever sphere, must be noble and may be great. My confident trust is in you.

GEORGE R.I.